# DEFINITIONS

***Leeward and Windward*** A boat's *le* she is head to wind, was away from t lee or directly downwind, her *leewar* lies. The other side is her *windward s overlap*, the one on the *leeward* sid other is the *windward* boat.

***Mark*** An object the sailing ins specified side, and a race committee vessei sun from which the starting or finishing line extends. An anchor line or an object attached accidentally to a *mark* is not part of it.

***Mark-Room*** *Room* for a boat to leave a *mark* on the required side. Also,

(a)  *room* to sail to the *mark* when her *proper course* is to sail close to it, and

(b)  *room* to round the *mark* as necessary to sail the course.

However, *mark-room* for a boat does not include *room* to tack unless she is *overlapped* inside and to *windward* of the boat required to give *mark-room* and she would be *fetching* the *mark* after her tack.

***Obstruction*** An object that a boat could not pass without changing course substantially, if she were sailing directly towards it and one of her hull lengths from it. An object that can be safely passed on only one side and an area so designated by the sailing instructions are also *obstructions*. However, a boat *racing* is not an *obstruction* to other boats unless they are required to *keep clear* of her or, if rule 23 applies, avoid her. A vessel under way, including a boat *racing*, is never a continuing *obstruction*.

***Overlap*** See ***Clear Astern*** and ***Clear Ahead; Overlap***.

***Party*** A *party* to a hearing is

(a)  for a protest hearing: a protestor, a protestee;

(b)  for a request for redress: a boat requesting redress or for which redress is requested, a race committee acting under rule 60.2(b), a technical committee acting under rule 60.4(b);

(c)  for a request for redress under rule 62.1(a): the body alleged to have made an improper action or omission;

(d)  a person against whom an allegation of a breach of rule 69 is made; a person presenting an allegation under rule 69;

(e)  a *support person* subject to a hearing under rule 60.3(d) or 69; any boat that person supports; a person appointed to present an allegation under rule 60.3(d).

However, the protest committee is never a *party*.

# DEFINITIONS

**Postpone** A *postponed* race is delayed before its scheduled start but may be started or *abandoned* later.

**Proper Course** A course a boat would sail to *finish* as soon as possible in the absence of the other boats referred to in the rule using the term. A boat has no *proper course* before her starting signal.

**Protest** An allegation made under rule 61.2 by a boat, a race committee, a technical committee or a protest committee that a boat has broken a *rule*.

**Racing** A boat is *racing* from her preparatory signal until she *finishes* and clears the finishing line and *marks* or retires, or until the race committee signals a general recall, *postponement* or *abandonment*.

**Room** The space a boat needs in the existing conditions, including space to comply with her obligations under the rules of Part 2 and rule 31, while manoeuvring promptly in a seamanlike way.

**Rule**

(a)    The rules in this book, including the Definitions, Race Signals, Introduction, preambles and the rules of relevant appendices, but not titles;

(b)    World Sailing Advertising Code, Anti-Doping Code, Betting and Anti-Corruption Code, Disciplinary Code, Eligibility Code, Sailor Classification Code, respectively Regulations 20, 21, 37, 35, 19 and 22;

(c)    the prescriptions of the national authority, unless they are changed by the notice of race or sailing instructions in compliance with the national authority's prescription, if any, to rule 88.2;

(d)    the class rules (for a boat racing under a handicap or rating system, the rules of that system are 'class rules');

(e)    the notice of race;

(f)    the sailing instructions; and

(g)    any other documents that govern the event.

**Start** A boat *starts* when, having been entirely on the pre-start side of the starting line at or after her starting signal, and having complied with rule 30.1 if it applies, any part of her hull, crew or equipment crosses the starting line in the direction of the first *mark*.

# DEFINITIONS

**Support Person**   Any person who

(a)  provides, or may provide, physical or advisory support to a competitor, including any coach, trainer, manager, team staff, medic, paramedic or any other person working with, treating or assisting a competitor in or preparing for the competition, or

(b)  is the parent or guardian of a competitor.

**Tack, Starboard or Port**   A boat is on the *tack*, *starboard* or *port*, corresponding to her *windward* side.

**Windward**   See **Leeward** and **Windward.**

**Zone**   The area around a *mark* within a distance of three hull lengths of the boat nearer to it. A boat is in the *zone* when any part of her hull is in the *zone*.

## Racing Charter

### Objectives

- To provide the framework for everyone to enjoy the sport of sailboat racing in whatever capacity and to whatever level the individual desires.

- To ensure that the sport of sailboat racing welcomes all people and treats them equally.

- To ensure that those who experience sailboat racing are encouraged to continue.

### Principles and Practices

- The sport welcomes all participants; it relies largely on self-compliance and self-policing. Those that deliberately take unfair advantage of this or behave in an inappropriate manner, either on or off the water, can expect action to be taken against them.

- Competitors agree to compete in compliance with the rules and behave in accordance with accepted standards of sailboat racing. When involved in a genuine dispute, all parties to the dispute and those deciding the matter will use the established procedures for achieving resolution.

- Foul or abusive language, intimidation, aggressive behaviour or lack of respect for others and their property will not be tolerated.

- Organizers, officials and other providers of sailboat racing agree to provide the fairest racing possible. This includes encouraging feed-back and facilitating the resolution of genuine disputes (including protests) in a timely and proper manner.

- Support persons agree to encourage their competitors to behave in compliance with the above principles and practices.

This Charter applies equally to those who organize, manage, coach, advise, judge, provide services and compete (including those who support competitors) in sailboat racing.

The RYA encourages the adoption and implementation of this Charter, and provides guidance and support to individuals and organizations to assist implementation. This guidance and support is consistent with the practices of World Sailing.

For further information, visit www.rya.org.uk/racingrules.

# APPLICATION OF RYA
# RACING CHARTER

*Through the Racing Charter, the RYA seeks to promote fair and enjoyable racing for all.*

**What competitors should expect**

- Racing that, as far as possible, is fair, enjoyable and safe.

- Shore facilities, administration and race management to acceptable standards and appropriate to the event.

- A way to complain or make a suggestion, and a response to complaints and suggestions.

- Prompt resolution of any disputes.

**What is expected of competitors, their coaches, managers and supporters**

- Courtesy and respect to other competitors, officials and other users of the water, both afloat and ashore.

- Compliance with the rules, and the taking of a penalty when required by the rules.

- Use of the provided services to resolve any disputes.

### Resolution of Racing Disputes

The RYA encourages the adoption of the Exoneration Penalty, Advisory Hearings and RYA Arbitration in addition to protest hearings to improve the understanding of and compliance with the Racing Rules of Sailing. See www.rya.org.uk/racingrules.

### Unacceptable Behaviour

The RYA encourages the use of rule 69 and rule 2 to penalise and deter unacceptable behaviour both on and off the water. Guidelines on their application in the UK are on page 200 of the RYA's Racing Rules of Sailing ('Misconduct').

## Safety – Recommended Triggers for Reporting to the RYA

Attention is drawn to recommended triggers for reporting accidents or injuries.

The RYA encourages reporting if an accident or injury involves any of the following:

- Fatality
- Hospitalisation required
- Statutory reporting to the MAIB
- If useful lessons can be learned
- If in doubt

This is mandatory if the accident or injury involves:

- An RYA organised racing event
- An RYA organised racing activity (including coaching and training)
- An RYA Recognised Training Centre

Further information can be found on the RYA website: www.rya.org.uk/knowledge-advice/safety-management/Pages/reporting.aspx

# CHANGES AND CORRECTIONS MADE BY WORLD SAILING
## AS AT JANUARY 2018

This reprint includes changes to the Racing Rules of Sailing (RRS) approved by World Sailing in November 2017 and effective from 1 January 2018, together with corrections to the RRS made since publication in July 2016. They are summarised below.

| | |
|---|---|
| **Definitions** | *Party (e)* changed |
| **Rule 63.1** | Changed |
| **Rule 63.9** | New rule added |
| **Rule 64.4** | Changed |
| **Appendix B** | Changed definition of *Proper Course* deleted |
| **Rule B2.17** | Corrected |
| **Rule E3.8** | Corrected |
| **Appendix G** | Table of National Sail Letters amended |
| **Appendix S** | Course diagrams corrected |

# The
# RACING RULES
## of
# SAILING

## for 2017 – 2020

**Including the RYA Prescriptions**

Royal Yachting Association
RYA House, Ensign Way, Hamble,
Southampton  SO31 4YA
Tel: 02380 604100
Email: publications@rya.org.uk
Website: www.rya.org.uk

© 2018 RYA

**The Royal Yachting Association**
RYA House, Ensign Way, Hamble,
Southampton  SO31 4YA
**Tel**:    02380 604100
**Email**: info@rya.org.uk
**Web**:  www.rya.org.uk
**ISBN**: 9781910017128
**RYA Order Code**: YR1/17
Reprinted January 2018

A CIP record of this book is available from
the British Library.

Note: While all reasonable care has been
taken in the preparation of this book, the
publisher takes no responsibility for the use
of the methods or products or contracts
described in the book.

Telephone 02380 604100 for a free copy of
our Publications Catalogue.

**Cover Design**: Creativebyte
**Typesetting**: Creativebyte
**Printed in China through**: World Print
**Photographic credits**: Richard Langdon,
onEdition, Paul Wyeth

© World Sailing Limited
June 2016

Published by the Royal Yachting Association
RYA website: www.rya.org.uk
© Royal Yachting Association, January 2018

# CONTENTS

# ONLINE RULES DOCUMENTS

*World Sailing has established a single internet address at which readers will find links to all the documents available on the World Sailing website that are mentioned in this book. Those documents are listed below. Links to other rules documents will also be provided at that address.*

*The address is: **sailing.org/racingrules/documents.***

# THE EQUIPMENT RULES
# OF SAILING

The World Sailing Equipment Rules of Sailing (ERS) are rules for the use of equipment in sailboat racing, equipment definitions, and rules on equipment control and inspection.

The ERS are not part of *The Racing Rules of Sailing*. They apply only when explicitly invoked by one or more of the following:

- Class rules or the rules of a rating system.

- The notice of race and sailing instructions for an event.

- National authority prescriptions.

The ERS are available in booklet form from World Sailing and they can be downloaded from www.sailing.org/ers.

# INTRODUCTION

*The Racing Rules of Sailing* includes two main sections. The first, Parts 1–7, contains rules that affect all competitors. The second, the appendices, provides details of rules, rules that apply to particular kinds of racing, and rules that affect only a small number of competitors or officials.

## Terminology

A term used in the sense stated in the Definitions is printed in italics or, in preambles, in bold italics (for example, *racing* and ***racing***).

Each of the terms in the table below is used in *The Racing Rules of Sailing* with the meaning given.

| Term | Meaning |
|------|---------|
| Boat | A sailboat and the crew on board. |
| Competitor | A person who races or intends to race in the event. |
| National authority | A World Sailing member national authority. |
| Race committee | The race committee appointed under rule 89.2(c) and any other person or committee performing a race committee function. |
| Racing rule | A rule in *The Racing Rules of Sailing*. |
| Technical committee | The technical committee appointed under rule 89.2(c) and any other person or committee performing a technical committee function. |
| Vessel | Any boat or ship. |

Other words and terms are used in the sense ordinarily understood in nautical or general use.

**Notation** The notation '[DP]' in a *rule* means that the penalty for a breach of the *rule* may, at the discretion of the protest committee, be less than disqualification. Guidelines for discretionary penalties are available on the World Sailing website.

**Revision** The racing rules are revised and published every four years by World Sailing, the international authority for the sport. This edition becomes effective on 1 January 2017 except that for an event beginning in 2016 the date may be postponed by the notice of race and sailing instructions. No changes are contemplated before 2021, but any changes determined to be urgent before then will be announced through national authorities and posted on the World Sailing website.

**Appendices**   When the rules of an appendix apply, they take precedence over any conflicting rules in Parts 1–7 and the Definitions. Each appendix is identified by a letter. A reference to a rule in an appendix will contain the letter and the rule number (for example, 'rule A1'). The letters I, O and Q are not used to designate appendices in this book.

**World Sailing Codes**   The World Sailing Codes are listed in the table below. The codes are published in the World Sailing Regulations.

| Title | Racing Rule | Regulation |
|---|---|---|
| Advertising Code | 80 | 20 |
| Anti-Doping Code | 5 | 21 |
| Betting and Anti-Corruption Code | 6 | 37 |
| Disciplinary Code | 7 | 35 |
| Eligibility Code | 75.2 | 19 |
| Sailor Classification Code | 79 | 22 |

These Codes are referred to in the definition *Rule* but are not included in this book because they can be changed at any time. The most recent versions of the codes are published on the World Sailing website; new versions will be announced through national authorities.

**Cases and Calls**   World Sailing publishes interpretations of the racing rules in *The Case Book for 2017–2020* and recognizes them as authoritative interpretations and explanations of the rules. It also publishes *The Call Book for Match Racing for 2017–2020* and *The Call Book for Team Racing for 2017–2020*, and it recognizes them as authoritative only for umpired match or team racing. These publications are available on the World Sailing website.

**Prescriptions**   The RYA prescriptions to the racing rules are printed on yellow pages 190–193. A rule with a prescription is marked with an RYA logo (**RYA**) in the margin. The RYA prescriptions may be changed only as stated in rule 88.2 and the RYA prescription to it.

---

The RYA will announce changes to the rules and World Sailing codes and will publish any changes to the RYA prescriptions on the RYA website (www.rya.org.uk/racingrules).

# BASIC PRINCIPLES

### SPORTSMANSHIP AND THE RULES

Competitors in the sport of sailing are governed by a body of *rules* that they are expected to follow and enforce. A fundamental principle of sportsmanship is that when competitors break a *rule* they will promptly take a penalty, which may be to retire.

### ENVIRONMENTAL RESPONSIBILITY

Participants are encouraged to minimize any adverse environmental impact of the sport of sailing.

# PART 1
## FUNDAMENTAL RULES

**1**      **SAFETY**
**1.1**    **Helping Those in Danger**
           A boat or competitor shall give all possible help to any person or
           vessel in danger.

**1.2**    **Life-Saving Equipment and Personal Flotation Devices**
           A boat shall carry adequate life-saving equipment for all persons on
           board, including one item ready for immediate use, unless her class
           rules make some other provision. Each competitor is individually
           responsible for wearing a personal flotation device adequate for the
           conditions.

**2**      **FAIR SAILING**
           A boat and her owner shall compete in compliance with recognized
           principles of sportsmanship and fair play. A boat may be penalized
           under this rule only if it is clearly established that these principles
           have been violated. The penalty shall be either disqualification or
           disqualification that is not excludable.

**RYA** **3**    **ACCEPTANCE OF THE RULES**
**3.1**    (a)  By participating or intending to participate in a race conducted
                under these *rules*, each competitor and boat owner agrees to
                accept these *rules*.
           (b)  A *support person* by providing support, or a parent or guardian
                by permitting their child to enter a race, agrees to accept the
                *rules*.

**3.2**    Each competitor and boat owner agrees, on behalf of their *support
           persons*, that such *support persons* are bound by the *rules*.

**3.3**    Acceptance of the *rules* includes agreement

           (a)  to be governed by the *rules*;

           (b)  to accept the penalties imposed and other action taken under
                the *rules*, subject to the appeal and review procedures provided
                in them, as the final determination of any matter arising under
                the *rules*;

    (c)    with respect to any such determination, not to resort to any court of law or tribunal not provided for in the *rules*; and

    (d)    by each competitor and boat owner to ensure that their *support persons* are aware of the *rules*.

**3.4**    The person in charge of each boat shall ensure that all competitors in the crew and the boat's owner are aware of their responsibilities under this rule.

**3.5**    This rule may be changed by a prescription of the national authority of the venue.

## 4    DECISION TO RACE

The responsibility for a boat's decision to participate in a race or to continue *racing* is hers alone.

## 5    ANTI-DOPING

A competitor shall comply with the World Anti-Doping Code, the rules of the World Anti-Doping Agency, and World Sailing Regulation 21, Anti-Doping Code. An alleged or actual breach of this rule shall be dealt with under Regulation 21. It shall not be grounds for a *protest* and rule 63.1 does not apply.

## 6    BETTING AND ANTI-CORRUPTION

Each competitor, boat owner and *support person* shall comply with World Sailing Regulation 37, Betting and Anti-Corruption Code. An alleged or actual breach of this rule shall be dealt with under Regulation 37. It shall not be grounds for a *protest* and rule 63.1 does not apply.

## 7    DISCIPLINARY CODE

Each competitor, boat owner and *support person* shall comply with World Sailing Regulation 35, Disciplinary, Appeals and Review Code (referred to as 'Disciplinary Code' elsewhere). An alleged or actual breach of this rule shall be dealt with under Regulation 35. It shall not be grounds for a *protest* and rule 63.1 does not apply.

# PART 2
## WHEN BOATS MEET

*The rules of Part 2 apply between boats that are sailing in or near the racing area and intend to **race**, are **racing**, or have been **racing**. However, a boat not **racing** shall not be penalized for breaking one of these rules, except rule 14 when the incident resulted in injury or serious damage, or rule 24.1.*

*When a boat sailing under these rules meets a vessel that is not, she shall comply with the* International Regulations for Preventing Collisions at Sea (IRPCAS) *or government right-of-way rules. If the sailing instructions so state, the rules of Part 2 are replaced by the right-of-way rules of the* IRPCAS *or by government right-of-way rules.*

### SECTION A
### RIGHT OF WAY

*A boat has right of way over another boat when the other boat is required to* **keep clear** *of her. However, some rules in Sections B, C and D limit the actions of a right-of-way boat.*

**10      ON OPPOSITE TACKS**

When boats are on opposite *tacks*, a *port-tack* boat shall *keep clear* of a *starboard-tack* boat.

**11      ON THE SAME TACK, OVERLAPPED**

When boats are on the same *tack* and *overlapped*, a *windward* boat shall *keep clear* of a *leeward* boat.

**12      ON THE SAME TACK, NOT OVERLAPPED**

When boats are on the same *tack* and not *overlapped*, a boat *clear astern* shall *keep clear* of a boat *clear ahead*.

**13      WHILE TACKING**

After a boat passes head to wind, she shall *keep clear* of other boats until she is on a close-hauled course. During that time rules 10, 11 and 12 do not apply. If two boats are subject to this rule at the same time, the one on the other's port side or the one astern shall *keep clear*.

## SECTION B
## GENERAL LIMITATIONS

**14**    **AVOIDING CONTACT**

A boat shall avoid contact with another boat if reasonably possible. However, a right-of-way boat or one entitled to *room* or *mark-room*

(a)    need not act to avoid contact until it is clear that the other boat is not *keeping clear* or giving *room* or *mark-room*, and

(b)    shall be exonerated if she breaks this rule and the contact does not cause damage or injury.

**15**    **ACQUIRING RIGHT OF WAY**

When a boat acquires right of way, she shall initially give the other boat *room* to *keep clear*, unless she acquires right of way because of the other boat's actions.

**16**    **CHANGING COURSE**

**16.1**    When a right-of-way boat changes course, she shall give the other boat *room* to *keep clear*.

**16.2**    In addition, when after the starting signal a *port-tack* boat is *keeping clear* by sailing to pass astern of a *starboard-tack* boat, the *starboard-tack* boat shall not change course if as a result the *port-tack* boat would immediately need to change course to continue *keeping clear*.

**17**    **ON THE SAME TACK; PROPER COURSE**

If a boat *clear astern* becomes *overlapped* within two of her hull lengths to *leeward* of a boat on the same *tack*, she shall not sail above her *proper course* while they remain on the same *tack* and *overlapped* within that distance, unless in doing so she promptly sails astern of the other boat. This rule does not apply if the *overlap* begins while the *windward* boat is required by rule 13 to *keep clear*.

## SECTION C
# AT MARKS AND OBSTRUCTIONS

*Section C rules do not apply at a starting **mark** surrounded by navigable water or at its anchor line from the time boats are approaching them to **start** until they have passed them.*

## 18      MARK-ROOM

### 18.1     When Rule 18 Applies

Rule 18 applies between boats when they are required to leave a *mark* on the same side and at least one of them is in the *zone*. However, it does not apply

(a) between boats on opposite *tacks* on a beat to windward,

(b) between boats on opposite *tacks* when the *proper course* at the *mark* for one but not both of them is to tack,

(c) between a boat approaching a *mark* and one leaving it, or

(d) if the *mark* is a continuing *obstruction*, in which case rule 19 applies.

### 18.2     Giving Mark-Room

(a) When boats are *overlapped* the outside boat shall give the inside boat *mark-room*, unless rule 18.2(b) applies.

(b) If boats are *overlapped* when the first of them reaches the *zone*, the outside boat at that moment shall thereafter give the inside boat *mark-room*. If a boat is *clear ahead* when she reaches the *zone*, the boat *clear astern* at that moment shall thereafter give her *mark-room*.

(c) When a boat is required to give *mark-room* by rule 18.2(b),

(1) she shall continue to do so even if later an *overlap* is broken or a new *overlap* begins;

(2) if she becomes *overlapped* inside the boat entitled to *mark-room*, she shall also give that boat *room* to sail her *proper course* while they remain *overlapped*.

(d) Rules 18.2(b) and (c) cease to apply when the boat entitled to *mark-room* has been given that *mark-room*, or if she passes head to wind or leaves the *zone*.

(e)    If there is reasonable doubt that a boat obtained or broke an *overlap* in time, it shall be presumed that she did not.

(f)    If a boat obtained an inside *overlap* from *clear astern* or by tacking to *windward* of the other boat and, from the time the *overlap* began, the outside boat has been unable to give *mark-room*, she is not required to give it.

**18.3    Tacking in the Zone**

If a boat in the *zone* of a *mark* to be left to port passes head to wind from *port* to *starboard tack* and is then *fetching* the *mark*, she shall not cause a boat that has been on *starboard tack* since entering the *zone* to sail above close-hauled to avoid contact and she shall give *mark-room* if that boat becomes *overlapped* inside her. When this rule applies between boats, rule 18.2 does not apply between them.

**18.4    Gybing**

When an inside *overlapped* right-of-way boat must gybe at a *mark* to sail her *proper course*, until she gybes she shall sail no farther from the *mark* than needed to sail that course. Rule 18.4 does not apply at a gate *mark*.

**19        ROOM TO PASS AN OBSTRUCTION**

**19.1    When Rule 19 Applies**

Rule 19 applies between two boats at an *obstruction* except

(a)    when the *obstruction* is a *mark* the boats are required to leave on the same side, or

(b)    when rule 18 applies between the boats and the *obstruction* is another boat *overlapped* with each of them.

However, at a continuing *obstruction*, rule 19 always applies and rule 18 does not.

**19.2    Giving Room at an Obstruction**

(a)    A right-of-way boat may choose to pass an *obstruction* on either side.

(b)    When boats are *overlapped*, the outside boat shall give the inside boat *room* between her and the *obstruction*, unless she has been unable to do so from the time the *overlap* began.

(c)    While boats are passing a continuing *obstruction*, if a boat that was *clear astern* and required to *keep clear* becomes *overlapped* between the other boat and the *obstruction* and, at the moment the *overlap* begins, there is not *room* for her to pass between them, she is not entitled to *room* under rule 19.2(b). While the boats remain *overlapped*, she shall *keep clear* and rules 10 and 11 do not apply.

## 20    ROOM TO TACK AT AN OBSTRUCTION

### 20.1    Hailing

A boat may hail for *room* to tack and avoid a boat on the same *tack*. However, she shall not hail unless

(a)    she is approaching an *obstruction* and will soon need to make a substantial course change to avoid it safely, and

(b)    she is sailing close-hauled or above.

In addition, she shall not hail if the *obstruction* is a *mark* and a boat that is *fetching* it would be required to change course as a result of the hail.

### 20.2    Responding

(a)    After a boat hails, she shall give a hailed boat time to respond.

(b)    A hailed boat shall respond even if the hail breaks rule 20.1.

(c)    A hailed boat shall respond either by tacking as soon as possible, or by immediately replying 'You tack' and then giving the hailing boat *room* to tack and avoid her.

(d)    When a hailed boat responds, the hailing boat shall tack as soon as possible.

(e)    From the time a boat hails until she has tacked and avoided a hailed boat, rule 18.2 does not apply between them.

### 20.3    Passing On a Hail to an Additional Boat

When a boat has been hailed for *room* to tack and she intends to respond by tacking, she may hail another boat on the same *tack* for *room* to tack and avoid her. She may hail even if her hail does not meet the conditions of rule 20.1. Rule 20.2 applies between her and a boat she hails.

# SECTION D
# OTHER RULES

*When rule 22 or 23 applies between two boats, Section A rules do not.*

**21    EXONERATION**

When a boat is sailing within the *room* or *mark-room* to which she is entitled, she shall be exonerated if, in an incident with a boat required to give her that *room* or *mark-room*,

(a)    she breaks a rule of Section A, rule 15 or rule 16, or

(b)    she is compelled to break rule 31.

**22    STARTING ERRORS; TAKING PENALTIES; BACKING A SAIL**

**22.1**    A boat sailing towards the pre-start side of the starting line or one of its extensions after her starting signal to *start* or to comply with rule 30.1 shall *keep clear* of a boat not doing so until she is completely on the pre-start side.

**22.2**    A boat taking a penalty shall *keep clear* of one that is not.

**22.3**    A boat moving astern, or sideways to windward, through the water by backing a sail shall *keep clear* of one that is not.

**23    CAPSIZED, ANCHORED OR AGROUND; RESCUING**

If possible, a boat shall avoid a boat that is capsized or has not regained control after capsizing, is anchored or aground, or is trying to help a person or vessel in danger. A boat is capsized when her masthead is in the water.

**24    INTERFERING WITH ANOTHER BOAT**

**24.1**    If reasonably possible, a boat not *racing* shall not interfere with a boat that is *racing*.

**24.2**    If reasonably possible, a boat shall not interfere with a boat that is taking a penalty, sailing on another leg or subject to rule 22.1. However, after the starting signal this rule does not apply when the boat is sailing her *proper course*.

# PART 3
## CONDUCT OF A RACE

**25**     **NOTICE OF RACE, SAILING INSTRUCTIONS AND SIGNALS**

**25.1**   The notice of race and sailing instructions shall be made available to each boat before a race begins.

**25.2**   The meanings of the visual and sound signals stated in Race Signals shall not be changed except under rule 86.1(b). The meanings of any other signals that may be used shall be stated in the notice of race or sailing instructions.

**25.3**   When the race committee is required to display a flag as a visual signal, it may use a flag or other object of a similar appearance.

**26**     **STARTING RACES**

Races shall be started by using the following signals. Times shall be taken from the visual signals; the absence of a sound signal shall be disregarded.

| Minutes before starting signal | Visual signal | Sound signal | Means |
|---|---|---|---|
| 5* | Class flag | One | Warning signal |
| 4 | P, I, Z, Z with I, U, or black flag | One | Preparatory signal |
| 1 | Preparatory flag removed | One long | One minute |
| 0 | Class flag removed | One | Starting signal |

*or as stated in the sailing instructions

The warning signal for each succeeding class shall be made with or after the starting signal of the preceding class.

## 27    OTHER RACE COMMITTEE ACTIONS BEFORE THE STARTING SIGNAL

**27.1**    No later than the warning signal, the race committee shall signal or otherwise designate the course to be sailed if the sailing instructions have not stated the course, and it may replace one course signal with another and signal that wearing personal flotation devices is required (display flag Y with one sound).

**27.2**    No later than the preparatory signal, the race committee may move a starting *mark*.

**27.3**    Before the starting signal, the race committee may for any reason *postpone* (display flag AP, AP over H, or AP over A, with two sounds) or *abandon* the race (display flag N over H, or N over A, with three sounds).

## 28    SAILING THE COURSE

**28.1**    A boat shall *start*, sail the course described in the sailing instructions and *finish*. While doing so, she may leave on either side a *mark* that does not begin, bound or end the leg she is sailing. After *finishing* she need not cross the finishing line completely.

**28.2**    A string representing a boat's track from the time she begins to approach the starting line from its pre-start side to *start* until she *finishes* shall, when drawn taut,

    (a)    pass each *mark* on the required side and in the correct order,

    (b)    touch each rounding *mark*, and

    (c)    pass between the *marks* of a gate from the direction of the previous *mark*.

She may correct any errors to comply with this rule, provided she has not *finished*.

## 29    RECALLS

### 29.1    Individual Recall

When at a boat's starting signal any part of her hull, crew or equipment is on the course side of the starting line or she must comply with rule 30.1, the race committee shall promptly display flag X with one sound. The flag shall be displayed until all such boats have sailed completely to the pre-start side of the starting line or one of its extensions and have complied with rule 30.1 if it applies, but no later than four minutes after the starting signal or one minute before any later starting signal, whichever is earlier. If rule 30.3 or 30.4 applies this rule does not.

## 29.2    General Recall

When at the starting signal the race committee is unable to identify boats that are on the course side of the starting line or to which rule 30 applies, or there has been an error in the starting procedure, the race committee may signal a general recall (display the First Substitute with two sounds). The warning signal for a new start for the recalled class shall be made one minute after the First Substitute is removed (one sound), and the starts for any succeeding classes shall follow the new start.

## 30    STARTING PENALTIES

## 30.1    I Flag Rule

If flag I has been displayed, and any part of a boat's hull, crew or equipment is on the course side of the starting line or one of its extensions during the last minute before her starting signal, she shall sail across an extension to the pre-start side before *starting*.

## 30.2    Z Flag Rule

If flag Z has been displayed, no part of a boat's hull, crew or equipment shall be in the triangle formed by the ends of the starting line and the first *mark* during the last minute before her starting signal. If a boat breaks this rule and is identified, she shall receive, without a hearing, a 20% Scoring Penalty calculated as stated in rule 44.3(c). She shall be penalized even if the race is restarted or resailed, but not if it is *postponed* or *abandoned* before the starting signal. If she is similarly identified during a subsequent attempt to start the same race, she shall receive an additional 20% Scoring Penalty.

## 30.3    U Flag Rule

If flag U has been displayed, no part of a boat's hull, crew or equipment shall be in the triangle formed by the ends of the starting line and the first *mark* during the last minute before her starting signal. If a boat breaks this rule and is identified, she shall be disqualified without a hearing, but not if the race is restarted or resailed.

### 30.4    Black Flag Rule

If a black flag has been displayed, no part of a boat's hull, crew or equipment shall be in the triangle formed by the ends of the starting line and the first *mark* during the last minute before her starting signal. If a boat breaks this rule and is identified, she shall be disqualified without a hearing, even if the race is restarted or resailed, but not if it is *postponed* or *abandoned* before the starting signal. If a general recall is signalled or the race is *abandoned* after the starting signal, the race committee shall display her sail number before the next warning signal for that race, and if the race is restarted or resailed she shall not sail in it. If she does so, her disqualification shall not be excluded in calculating her series score.

### 31    TOUCHING A MARK

While *racing*, a boat shall not touch a starting *mark* before *starting*, a *mark* that begins, bounds or ends the leg of the course on which she is sailing, or a finishing *mark* after *finishing*.

### 32    SHORTENING OR ABANDONING AFTER THE START

### 32.1

After the starting signal, the race committee may shorten the course (display flag S with two sounds) or *abandon* the race (display flag N, N over H, or N over A, with three sounds),

(a)    because of foul weather,

(b)    because of insufficient wind making it unlikely that any boat will *finish* within the time limit,

(c)    because a *mark* is missing or out of position, or

(d)    for any other reason directly affecting the safety or fairness of the competition.

In addition, the race committee may shorten the course so that other scheduled races can be sailed, or *abandon* the race because of an error in the starting procedure. However, after one boat has sailed the course and *finished* within the time limit, if any, the race committee shall not *abandon* the race without considering the consequences for all boats in the race or series.

**32.2**    If the race committee signals a shortened course (displays flag S with two sounds), the finishing line shall be,

(a)    at a rounding *mark*, between the *mark* and a staff displaying flag S;

(b)    a line the course requires boats to cross; or

(c)    at a gate, between the gate *marks*.

The shortened course shall be signalled before the first boat crosses the finishing line.


**33    CHANGING THE NEXT LEG OF THE COURSE**

The race committee may change a leg of the course that begins at a rounding *mark* or at a gate by changing the position of the next *mark* (or the finishing line) and signalling all boats before they begin the leg. The next *mark* need not be in position at that time.

(a)    If the direction of the leg will be changed, the signal shall be the display of flag C with repetitive sounds and one or both of

(1)    the new compass bearing,

(2)    a green triangle for a change to starboard or a red rectangle for a change to port.

(b)    If the length of the leg will be changed, the signal shall be the display of flag C with repetitive sounds and a '−' if the length will be decreased or a '+' if it will be increased.

(c)    Subsequent legs may be changed without further signalling to maintain the course shape.


**34    MARK MISSING**

If a *mark* is missing or out of position, the race committee shall, if possible,

a)    replace it in its correct position or substitute a new one of similar appearance, or

(b)    substitute an object displaying flag M and make repetitive sound signals.

**35      TIME LIMIT AND SCORES**

If one boat sails the course as required by rule 28 and *finishes* within the time limit, if any, all boats that *finish* shall be scored according to their finishing places unless the race is *abandoned*. If no boat *finishes* within the time limit, the race committee shall *abandon* the race.

**36      RACES RESTARTED OR RESAILED**

If a race is restarted or resailed, a breach of a *rule* in the original race, or in any previous restart or resail of that race, shall not

(a)    prohibit a boat from competing unless she has broken rule 30.4; or

(b)    cause a boat to be penalized except under rule 30.2, 30.4 or 69 or under rule 14 when she has caused injury or serious damage.

# PART 4
# OTHER REQUIREMENTS WHEN RACING

*Part 4 rules apply only to boats **racing** unless the rule states otherwise.*

**R̸A 40**  **PERSONAL FLOTATION DEVICES**

When flag Y is displayed with one sound before or with the warning signal, competitors shall wear personal flotation devices, except briefly while changing or adjusting clothing or personal equipment. When flag Y is displayed ashore, this rule applies at all times while afloat. Wet suits and dry suits are not personal flotation devices.

**41**  **OUTSIDE HELP**

A boat shall not receive help from any outside source, except

(a)  help for a crew member who is ill, injured or in danger;

(b)  after a collision, help from the crew of the other vessel to get clear;

(c)  help in the form of information freely available to all boats;

(d)  unsolicited information from a disinterested source, which may be another boat in the same race.

However, a boat that gains a significant advantage in the race from help received under rule 41(a) may be protested and penalized; any penalty may be less than disqualification.

**42**  **PROPULSION**

**42.1**  **Basic Rule**

Except when permitted in rule 42.3 or 45, a boat shall compete by using only the wind and water to increase, maintain or decrease her speed. Her crew may adjust the trim of sails and hull, and perform other acts of seamanship, but shall not otherwise move their bodies to propel the boat.

## 42.2    Prohibited Actions

Without limiting the application of rule 42.1, these actions are prohibited:

(a)    pumping: repeated fanning of any sail either by pulling in and releasing the sail or by vertical or athwartship body movement;

(b)    rocking: repeated rolling of the boat, induced by

   (1)    body movement,

   (2)    repeated adjustment of the sails or centreboard, or

   (3)    steering;

(c)    ooching: sudden forward body movement, stopped abruptly;

(d)    sculling: repeated movement of the helm that is either forceful or that propels the boat forward or prevents her from moving astern;

(e)    repeated tacks or gybes unrelated to changes in the wind or to tactical considerations.

## 42.3    Exceptions

(a)    A boat may be rolled to facilitate steering.

(b)    A boat's crew may move their bodies to exaggerate the rolling that facilitates steering the boat through a tack or a gybe, provided that, just after the tack or gybe is completed, the boat's speed is not greater than it would have been in the absence of the tack or gybe.

(c)    Except on a beat to windward, when surfing (rapidly accelerating down the front of a wave) or planing is possible, the boat's crew may pull in any sail in order to initiate surfing or planing, but each sail may be pulled in only once for each wave or gust of wind.

(d)    When a boat is above a close-hauled course and either stationary or moving slowly, she may scull to turn to a close-hauled course.

(e)    If a batten is inverted, the boat's crew may pump the sail until the batten is no longer inverted. This action is not permitted if it clearly propels the boat.

(f)    A boat may reduce speed by repeatedly moving her helm.

(g)  Any means of propulsion may be used to help a person or another vessel in danger.

(h)  To get clear after grounding or colliding with a vessel or object, a boat may use force applied by her crew or the crew of the other vessel and any equipment other than a propulsion engine. However, the use of an engine may be permitted by rule 42.3(i).

(i)  Sailing instructions may, in stated circumstances, permit propulsion using an engine or any other method, provided the boat does not gain a significant advantage in the race.

*Note: Interpretations of rule 42 are available at the World Sailing website or by mail upon request.*

## 43    COMPETITOR CLOTHING AND EQUIPMENT

**43.1**  (a)  Competitors shall not wear or carry clothing or equipment for the purpose of increasing their weight.

(b)  Furthermore, a competitor's clothing and equipment shall not weigh more than 8 kilograms, excluding a hiking or trapeze harness and clothing (including footwear) worn only below the knee. Class rules or sailing instructions may specify a lower weight or a higher weight up to 10 kilograms. Class rules may include footwear and other clothing worn below the knee within that weight. A hiking or trapeze harness shall have positive buoyancy and shall not weigh more than 2 kilograms, except that class rules may specify a higher weight up to 4 kilograms. Weights shall be determined as required by Appendix H.

**43.2**  Rule 43.1(b) does not apply to boats required to be equipped with lifelines.

## 44    PENALTIES AT THE TIME OF AN INCIDENT

### 44.1    Taking a Penalty

A boat may take a Two-Turns Penalty when she may have broken one or more rules of Part 2 in an incident while *racing*. She may take a One-Turn Penalty when she may have broken rule 31. Alternatively, sailing instructions may specify the use of the Scoring

Penalty or some other penalty, in which case the specified penalty shall replace the One-Turn and the Two-Turns Penalty. However,

(a)    when a boat may have broken a rule of Part 2 and rule 31 in the same incident she need not take the penalty for breaking rule 31;

(b)    if the boat caused injury or serious damage or, despite taking a penalty, gained a significant advantage in the race or series by her breach her penalty shall be to retire.

**44.2    One-Turn and Two-Turns Penalties**

After getting well clear of other boats as soon after the incident as possible, a boat takes a One-Turn or Two-Turns Penalty by promptly making the required number of turns in the same direction, each turn including one tack and one gybe. When a boat takes the penalty at or near the finishing line, she shall sail completely to the course side of the line before *finishing*.

**44.3    Scoring Penalty**

(a)    A boat takes a Scoring Penalty by displaying a yellow flag at the first reasonable opportunity after the incident.

(b)    When a boat has taken a Scoring Penalty, she shall keep the yellow flag displayed until *finishing* and call the race committee's attention to it at the finishing line. At that time she shall also inform the race committee of the identity of the other boat involved in the incident. If this is impracticable, she shall do so at the first reasonable opportunity and within the protest time limit.

(c)    The race score for a boat that takes a Scoring Penalty shall be the score she would have received without that penalty, made worse by the number of places stated in the sailing instructions. When the sailing instructions do not state the number of places, the penalty shall be 20% of the score for Did Not *Finish*, rounded to the nearest whole number (0.5 rounded upward). The scores of other boats shall not be changed; therefore, two boats may receive the same score. However, the penalty shall not cause the boat's score to be worse than the score for Did Not *Finish*.

## 45    HAULING OUT; MAKING FAST; ANCHORING

A boat shall be afloat and off moorings at her preparatory signal. Thereafter, she shall not be hauled out or made fast except to bail out, reef sails or make repairs. She may anchor or the crew may stand on the bottom. She shall recover the anchor before continuing in the race unless she is unable to do so.

## 46    PERSON IN CHARGE

A boat shall have on board a person in charge designated by the member or organization that entered the boat. See rule 75.

## 47    LIMITATIONS ON EQUIPMENT AND CREW

**47.1**    A boat shall use only the equipment on board at her preparatory signal.

**47.2**    No person on board shall intentionally leave, except when ill or injured, or to help a person or vessel in danger, or to swim. A person leaving the boat by accident or to swim shall be back on board before the boat continues in the race.

## 48    FOG SIGNALS AND LIGHTS; TRAFFIC SEPARATION SCHEMES

**48.1**    When safety requires, a boat shall sound fog signals and show lights as required by the *International Regulations for Preventing Collisions at Sea (IRPCAS)* or applicable government rules.

**48.2**    A boat shall comply with rule 10, Traffic Separation Schemes, of the *IRPCAS*.

## 49    CREW POSITION; LIFELINES

**49.1**    Competitors shall use no device designed to position their bodies outboard, other than hiking straps and stiffeners worn under the thighs.

**49.2**    When lifelines are required by the class rules or any other *rule*, competitors shall not position any part of their torsos outside them, except briefly to perform a necessary task. On boats equipped with upper and lower lifelines, a competitor sitting on the deck facing outboard with his waist inside the lower lifeline may have the upper part of his body outside the upper lifeline. Unless a class rule or any other *rule* specifies a maximum deflection, lifelines shall be taut. If the class rules do not specify the material or minimum diameter of lifelines, they shall comply with the corresponding specifications in the *World Sailing Offshore Special Regulations*.

*Note: Those regulations are available at the World Sailing website.*

## 50    SETTING AND SHEETING SAILS

### 50.1    Changing Sails

When headsails or spinnakers are being changed, a replacing sail may be fully set and trimmed before the replaced sail is lowered. However, only one mainsail and, except when changing, only one spinnaker shall be carried set at a time.

### 50.2    Spinnaker Poles; Whisker Poles

Only one spinnaker pole or whisker pole shall be used at a time except when gybing. When in use, it shall be attached to the foremost mast.

### 50.3    Use of Outriggers

(a) No sail shall be sheeted over or through an outrigger, except as permitted in rule 50.3(b) or 50.3(c). An outrigger is any fitting or other device so placed that it could exert outward pressure on a sheet or sail at a point from which, with the boat upright, a vertical line would fall outside the hull or deck. For the purpose of this rule, bulwarks, rails and rubbing strakes are not part of the hull or deck and the following are not outriggers: a bowsprit used to secure the tack of a sail, a bumkin used to sheet the boom of a sail, or a boom of a boomed headsail that requires no adjustment when tacking.

(b) Any sail may be sheeted to or led above a boom that is regularly used for a sail and is permanently attached to the mast from which the head of the sail is set.

(c) A headsail may be sheeted or attached at its clew to a spinnaker pole or whisker pole, provided that a spinnaker is not set.

**RYA** 50.4    **Headsails**

For the purposes of rules 50 and 54 and Appendix G, the difference between a headsail and a spinnaker is that the width of a headsail, measured between the midpoints of its luff and leech, is less than 75% of the length of its foot. A sail tacked down behind the foremost mast is not a headsail.

51    **MOVABLE BALLAST**

All movable ballast, including sails that are not set, shall be properly stowed. Water, dead weight or ballast shall not be moved for the purpose of changing trim or stability. Floorboards, bulkheads, doors, stairs and water tanks shall be left in place and all cabin fixtures kept on board. However, bilge water may be bailed out.

52    **MANUAL POWER**

A boat's standing rigging, running rigging, spars and movable hull appendages shall be adjusted and operated only by the power provided by the crew.

53    **SKIN FRICTION**

A boat shall not eject or release a substance, such as a polymer, or have specially textured surfaces that could improve the character of the flow of water inside the boundary layer.

54    **FORESTAYS AND HEADSAIL TACKS**

Forestays and headsail tacks, except those of spinnaker staysails when the boat is not close-hauled, shall be attached approximately on a boat's centreline.

55    **TRASH DISPOSAL**

A competitor shall not intentionally put trash in the water. This rule applies at all times while afloat. The penalty for a breach of this rule may be less than disqualification.

# PART 5
# PROTESTS, REDRESS, HEARINGS, MISCONDUCT AND APPEALS

## SECTION A
## PROTESTS; REDRESS; RULE 69 ACTION

**60**  **RIGHT TO PROTEST; RIGHT TO REQUEST REDRESS OR RULE 69 ACTION**

**60.1**  A boat may

(a)  protest another boat, but not for an alleged breach of a rule of Part 2 or rule 31 unless she was involved in or saw the incident; or

(b)  request redress.

**60.2**  A race committee may

(a)  protest a boat, but not as a result of information arising from a request for redress or an invalid *protest*, or from a report from a person with a *conflict of interest* other than the representative of the boat herself;

(b)  request redress for a boat; or

(c)  report to the protest committee requesting action under rule 69.2(b).

**60.3**  A protest committee may

(a)  protest a boat, but not as a result of information arising from a request for redress or an invalid *protest*, or from a report from a person with a *conflict of interest* other than the representative of the boat herself. However, it may protest a boat

(1)  if it learns of an incident involving her that may have resulted in injury or serious damage, or

(2)  if during the hearing of a valid *protest* it learns that the boat, although not a *party* to the hearing, was involved in the incident and may have broken a *rule*;

(b)  call a hearing to consider redress;

    (c)   act under rule 69.2(b); or

    (d)   call a hearing to consider whether a *support person* has broken a *rule*, based on its own observation or information received from any source, including evidence taken during a hearing.

**60.4**    A technical committee may

    (a)   protest a boat, but not as a result of information arising from a request for redress or an invalid *protest*, or from a report from a person with a *conflict of interest* other than the representative of the boat herself. However, it shall protest a boat if it decides that

        (1)   a boat has broken a rule of Part 4, but not rules 41, 42, 44 and 46, or

        (2)   a boat or personal equipment does not comply with the class rules;

    (b)   request redress for a boat; or

    (c)   report to the protest committee requesting action under rule 69.2(b).

**60.5**    However, neither a boat nor a committee may protest for an alleged breach of rule 5, 6, 7 or 69.

## 61    PROTEST REQUIREMENTS

### 61.1    Informing the Protestee

    (a)   A boat intending to protest shall inform the other boat at the first reasonable opportunity. When her *protest* will concern an incident in the racing area that she was involved in or saw, she shall hail 'Protest' and conspicuously display a red flag at the first reasonable opportunity for each. She shall display the flag until she is no longer *racing*. However,

        (1)   if the other boat is beyond hailing distance, the protesting boat need not hail but she shall inform the other boat at the first reasonable opportunity;

        (2)   if the hull length of the protesting boat is less than 6 metres, she need not display a red flag;

        (3)   if the incident was an error by the other boat in sailing the course, she need not hail or display a red flag but she shall inform the other boat either before or at the first reasonable opportunity after the other boat *finishes*;

(4)    if as a result of the incident a member of either crew is in danger, or there is injury or serious damage that is obvious to the boat intending to protest, the requirements of this rule do not apply to her, but she shall attempt to inform the other boat within the time limit of rule 61.3.

(b)    If the race committee, technical committee or protest committee intends to protest a boat concerning an incident the committee observed in the racing area, it shall inform her after the race within the time limit of rule 61.3. In other cases the committee shall inform the boat of its intention to protest as soon as reasonably possible.

(c)    If the protest committee decides to protest a boat under rule 60.3(a)(2), it shall inform her as soon as reasonably possible, close the current hearing, proceed as required by rules 61.2 and 63, and hear the original and the new *protests* together.

## 61.2    Protest Contents

A *protest* shall be in writing and identify

(a)    the protestor and protestee;

(b)    the incident;

(c)    where and when the incident occurred;

(d)    any *rule* the protestor believes was broken; and

(e)    the name of the protestor's representative.

However, if requirement (b) is met, requirement (a) may be met at any time before the hearing, and requirements (d) and (e) may be met before or during the hearing. Requirement (c) may also be met before or during the hearing, provided the protestee is allowed reasonable time to prepare for the hearing.

## 61.3    Protest Time Limit

A *protest* by a boat, or by the race committee, technical committee or protest committee about an incident the committee observed in the racing area, shall be delivered to the race office within the protest time limit stated in the sailing instructions. If none is stated, the time limit is two hours after the last boat in the race *finishes*. Other race committee, technical committee or protest committee *protests* shall be delivered to the race office no later than two hours after the committee receives the relevant information. The protest committee shall extend the time if there is good reason to do so.

**62      REDRESS**

**62.1**    A request for redress or a protest committee's decision to consider redress shall be based on a claim or possibility that a boat's score or place in a race or series has been or may be, through no fault of her own, made significantly worse by

(a)    an improper action or omission of the race committee, protest committee, organizing authority or technical committee for the event, but not by a protest committee decision when the boat was a *party* to the hearing;

(b)    injury or physical damage because of the action of a boat that was breaking a rule of Part 2 or of a vessel not *racing* that was required to keep clear;

(c)    giving help (except to herself or her crew) in compliance with rule 1.1; or

(d)    an action of a boat, or a member of her crew, that resulted in a penalty under rule 2 or a penalty or warning under rule 69.2(h).

**62.2**    A request shall be in writing and identify the reason for making it. If the request is based on an incident in the racing area, it shall be delivered to the race office within the protest time limit or two hours after the incident, whichever is later. Other requests shall be delivered as soon as reasonably possible after learning of the reasons for making the request. The protest committee shall extend the time if there is good reason to do so. No red flag is required.

# SECTION B
# HEARINGS AND DECISIONS

**63      HEARINGS**

**63.1    Requirement for a Hearing**

A boat or competitor shall not be penalized without a protest hearing, except as provided in rules 30.2, 30.3, 30.4, 64.3(d), 64.4(b), 69, 78.2, A5 and P2. A decision on redress shall not be made without a hearing. The protest committee shall hear all *protests* and requests for redress that have been delivered to the race office unless it allows a *protest* or request to be withdrawn.

## 63.2    Time and Place of the Hearing; Time for Parties to Prepare

All *parties* to the hearing shall be notified of the time and place of the hearing, the *protest* or redress information shall be made available to them, and they shall be allowed reasonable time to prepare for the hearing.

## 63.3    Right to Be Present

(a) A representative of each *party* to the hearing has the right to be present throughout the hearing of all the evidence. When a *protest* claims a breach of a rule of Part 2, 3 or 4, the representatives of boats shall have been on board at the time of the incident, unless there is good reason for the protest committee to rule otherwise. Any witness, other than a member of the protest committee, shall be excluded except when giving evidence.

(b) If a *party* to the hearing of a *protest* or request for redress does not come to the hearing, the protest committee may nevertheless decide the *protest* or request. If the *party* was unavoidably absent, the committee may reopen the hearing.

## 63.4    Conflict of Interest

(a) A protest committee member shall declare any possible *conflict of interest* as soon as he is aware of it. A *party* to the hearing who believes a member of the protest committee has a *conflict of interest* shall object as soon as possible. A *conflict of interest* declared by a protest committee member shall be included in the written information provided under rule 65.2.

(b) A member of a protest committee with a *conflict of interest* shall not be a member of the committee for the hearing, unless

(1) all *parties* consent, or

(2) the protest committee decides that the *conflict of interest* is not significant.

(c) When deciding whether a *conflict of interest* is significant, the protest committee shall consider the views of the *parties*, the level of the conflict, the level of the event, the importance to each *party*, and the overall perception of fairness.

(d)    However, for World Sailing major events, or for other events as prescribed by the national authority of the venue, rule 63.4(b) does not apply and a person who has a *conflict of interest* shall not be a member of the protest committee.

### 63.5    Validity of the Protest or Request for Redress

At the beginning of the hearing the protest committee shall take any evidence it considers necessary to decide whether all requirements for the *protest* or request for redress have been met. If they have been met, the *protest* or request is valid and the hearing shall be continued. If not, the committee shall declare the *protest* or request invalid and close the hearing. If the *protest* has been made under rule 60.3(a)(1), the committee shall also determine whether or not injury or serious damage resulted from the incident in question. If not, the hearing shall be closed.

### 63.6    Taking Evidence and Finding Facts

The protest committee shall take the evidence of the *parties* present at the hearing and of their witnesses and other evidence it considers necessary. A member of the protest committee who saw the incident shall, while the *parties* are present, state that fact and may give evidence. A *party* present at the hearing may question any person who gives evidence. The committee shall then find the facts and base its decision on them.

### 63.7    Conflict Between Rules

If there is a conflict between two or more *rules* that must be resolved before the protest committee makes a decision, the committee shall apply the *rule* that it believes will provide the fairest result for all boats affected. Rule 63.7 applies only if the conflict is between rules in the notice of race, the sailing instructions, or any of the other documents that govern the event under item (g) of the definition *Rule*.

### 63.8    Protests Between Boats in Different Races

A *protest* between boats sailing in different races conducted by different organizing authorities shall be heard by a protest committee acceptable to those authorities.

**63.9    Hearings under Rule 60.3(d) – Support Persons**

If the protest committee decides to call a hearing under rule 60.3(d), it shall promptly follow the procedures in rules 63.2, 63.3, 63.4 and 63.6, except that the information given to the *parties* shall be details of the alleged breach and a person may be appointed by the protest committee to present the allegation.

**64    DECISIONS**

**64.1    Penalties and Exoneration**

When the protest committee decides that a boat that is a *party* to a protest hearing has broken a *rule* and is not exonerated, it shall disqualify her unless some other penalty applies. A penalty shall be imposed whether or not the applicable *rule* was mentioned in the *protest*. If a boat has broken a *rule* when not *racing*, her penalty shall apply to the race sailed nearest in time to that of the incident. However,

(a)    when as a consequence of breaking a *rule* a boat has compelled another boat to break a *rule*, the other boat shall be exonerated.

(b)    if a boat has taken an applicable penalty, she shall not be further penalized under this rule unless the penalty for a *rule* she broke is a disqualification that is not excludable from her series score.

(c)    if the race is restarted or resailed, rule 36 applies.

**64.2    Decisions on Redress**

When the protest committee decides that a boat is entitled to redress under rule 62, it shall make as fair an arrangement as possible for all boats affected, whether or not they asked for redress. This may be to adjust the scoring (see rule A10 for some examples) or finishing times of boats, to *abandon* the race, to let the results stand or to make some other arrangement. When in doubt about the facts or probable results of any arrangement for the race or series, especially before *abandoning* the race, the protest committee shall take evidence from appropriate sources.

**64.3    Decisions on Protests Concerning Class Rules**

(a)    When the protest committee finds that deviations in excess of tolerances specified in the class rules were caused by damage or normal wear and do not improve the performance of the boat, it shall not penalize her. However, the boat shall not *race* again until the deviations have been corrected, except when the protest committee decides there is or has been no reasonable opportunity to do so.

(b)   When the protest committee is in doubt about the meaning of a class rule, it shall refer its questions, together with the relevant facts, to an authority responsible for interpreting the rule. In making its decision, the committee shall be bound by the reply of the authority.

(c)   When a boat is penalized under a class rule and the protest committee decides that the boat also broke the same rule in earlier races in the same event, the penalty may be imposed for all such races. No further *protest* is necessary.

(d)   When a boat penalized under a class rule states in writing that she intends to appeal, she may compete in subsequent races without changes to the boat. However, if she fails to appeal or the appeal is decided against her, she shall be disqualified without a further hearing from all subsequent races in which she competed.

(e)   Measurement costs arising from a *protest* involving a class rule shall be paid by the unsuccessful *party* unless the protest committee decides otherwise.

**64.4   Decisions Concerning Support Persons**

(a)   When the protest committee decides that a *support person* who is a *party* to a hearing under rule 60.3(d) or 69 has broken a *rule*, it may

(1)   issue a warning,

(2)   exclude the person from the event or venue or remove any privileges or benefits, or

(3)   take other action within its jurisdiction as provided by the *rules*.

(b)   The protest committee may also penalize a boat that is a *party* to a hearing under rule 60.3(d) or 69 for the breach of a *rule* by a *support person* by changing the boat's score in a single race, up to and including DSQ, when the protest committee decides that

(1)   the boat may have gained a competitive advantage as the result of the breach by the *support person*, or

(2)   the *support person* committed a further breach after the protest committee warned the boat in writing, following a previous hearing, that a penalty may be imposed.

## 65    INFORMING THE PARTIES AND OTHERS

**65.1**    After making its decision, the protest committee shall promptly inform the *parties* to the hearing of the facts found, the applicable *rules*, the decision, the reasons for it, and any penalties imposed or redress given.

**65.2**    A *party* to the hearing is entitled to receive the above information in writing, provided she asks for it in writing from the protest committee no later than seven days after being informed of the decision. The committee shall then promptly provide the information, including, when relevant, a diagram of the incident prepared or endorsed by the committee.

**65.3**    When the protest committee penalizes a boat under a class rule, it shall send the above information to the relevant class rule authorities.

## 66    REOPENING A HEARING

The protest committee may reopen a hearing when it decides that it may have made a significant error, or when significant new evidence becomes available within a reasonable time. It shall reopen a hearing when required by the national authority under rule 71.2 or R5. A *party* to the hearing may ask for a reopening no later than 24 hours after being informed of the decision. On the last scheduled day of racing the request shall be delivered

(a)    within the protest time limit if the requesting *party* was informed of the decision on the previous day;

(b)    no later than 30 minutes after the *party* was informed of the decision on that day.

When a hearing is reopened, a majority of the members of the protest committee shall, if possible, be members of the original protest committee.

## ▓A 67    DAMAGES

The question of damages arising from a breach of any *rule* shall be governed by the prescriptions, if any, of the national authority.

*Note: There is no rule 68.*

## SECTION C
# MISCONDUCT

**69      MISCONDUCT**

**69.1      Obligation not to Commit Misconduct; Resolution**

(a)   A competitor, boat owner or *support person* shall not commit an act of misconduct.

(b)   Misconduct is:

(1)   conduct that is a breach of good manners, a breach of good sportsmanship, or unethical behaviour; or

(2)    conduct that may bring the sport into disrepute.

(c)   An allegation of a breach of rule 69.1(a) shall be resolved in accordance with the provisions of rule 69. It shall not be grounds for a *protest* and rule 63.1 does not apply.

**69.2      Action by a Protest Committee**

(a)   A protest committee acting under this rule shall have at least three members.

(b)   When a protest committee, from its own observation or from information received from any source, including evidence taken during a hearing, believes a person may have broken rule 69.1(a), it shall decide whether or not to call a hearing.

(c)   When the protest committee needs more information to make the decision to call a hearing, it shall consider appointing a person or persons to conduct an investigation. These investigators shall not be members of the protest committee that will decide the matter.

(d)   When an investigator is appointed, all relevant information he gathers, favourable or unfavourable, shall be disclosed to the protest committee, and if the protest committee decides to call a hearing, to the *parties*.

(e) If the protest committee decides to call a hearing, it shall promptly inform the person in writing of the alleged breach and of the time and place of the hearing and follow the procedures in rules 63.2, 63.3(a), 63.4 and 63.6 except that:

  (1) unless a person has been appointed by World Sailing, a person may be appointed by the protest committee to present the allegation.

  (2) a person against whom an allegation has been made under this rule shall be entitled to have an advisor and a representative with him who may act on his behalf.

(f) If the person is unable to attend the hearing and

  (1) provides good reason, the protest committee shall reschedule it; or

  (2) does not provide good reason and does not come to it, the protest committee may conduct it without the person present.

(g) The standard of proof to be applied is the test of the comfortable satisfaction of the protest committee, bearing in mind the seriousness of the alleged misconduct. However, if the standard of proof in this rule conflicts with the laws of a country, the national authority may, with the approval of World Sailing, change it with a prescription to this rule.

(h) When the protest committee decides that a competitor or boat owner has broken rule 69.1(a), it may take one or more of the following actions

  (1) issue a warning;

  (2) change their boat's score in one or more races, including disqualification(s) that may or may not be excluded from her series score;

  (3) exclude the person from the event or venue or remove any privileges or benefits; and

  (4) take any other action within its jurisdiction as provided by the *rules*.

(i) When the protest committee decides that a *support person* has broken rule 69.1(a), rule 64.4 applies.

(j)   If the protest committee

    (1)   imposes a penalty greater than one DNE;

    (2)   excludes the person from the event or venue; or

    (3)   in any other case if it considers it appropriate,

it shall report its findings, including the facts found, its conclusions and decision to the national authority of the person or, for specific international events listed in the World Sailing Regulations, to World Sailing. If the protest committee has acted under rule 69.2(f)(2), the report shall also include that fact and the reasons for it.

(k)   If the protest committee decides not to conduct the hearing without the person present, or if the protest committee has left the event and a report alleging a breach of rule 69.1(a) is received, the race committee or organizing authority may appoint the same or a new protest committee to proceed under this rule. If it is impractical for the protest committee to conduct a hearing, it shall collect all available information and, if the allegation seems justified, make a report to the national authority of the person or, for specific international events listed in the World Sailing Regulations, to World Sailing.

**69.3    Action by a National Authority and World Sailing**

The disciplinary powers, procedures and responsibilities of national authorities and World Sailing that apply are specified in World Sailing Regulation 35, Disciplinary Code. National authorities and World Sailing may impose further penalties, including suspension of eligibility, under that regulation.

# SECTION D
# APPEALS

**70    APPEALS AND REQUESTS TO A NATIONAL AUTHORITY**

**70.1**   (a)   Provided that the right of appeal has not been denied under rule 70.5, a *party* to a hearing may appeal a protest committee's decision or its procedures, but not the facts found.

(b)   A boat may appeal when she is denied a hearing required by rule 63.1.

**70.2**    A protest committee may request confirmation or correction of its decision.

**70.3**    An appeal under rule 70.1 or a request by a protest committee under rule 70.2 shall be sent to the national authority with which the organizing authority is associated under rule 89.1. However, if boats will pass through the waters of more than one national authority while *racing*, the sailing instructions shall identify the national authority to which appeals or requests are required to be sent.

**70.4**    A club or other organization affiliated to a national authority may request an interpretation of the *rules*, provided that no *protest* or request for redress that may be appealed is involved. The interpretation shall not be used for changing a previous protest committee decision.

**70.5**    There shall be no appeal from the decisions of an international jury constituted in compliance with Appendix N. Furthermore, if the notice of race and the sailing instructions so state, the right of appeal may be denied provided that

(a)    it is essential to determine promptly the result of a race that will qualify a boat to compete in a later stage of an event or a subsequent event (a national authority may prescribe that its approval is required for such a procedure);

(b)    a national authority so approves for a particular event open only to entrants under its own jurisdiction; or

(c)    a national authority after consultation with World Sailing so approves for a particular event, provided the protest committee is constituted as required by Appendix N, except that only two members of the protest committee need be International Judges.

**70.6**    Appeals and requests shall conform to Appendix R.

**71**    **NATIONAL AUTHORITY DECISIONS**

**71.1**    A person who has a *conflict of interest* or was a member of the protest committee shall not take any part in the discussion or decision on an appeal or a request for confirmation or correction.

**71.2**   The national authority may uphold, change or reverse a protest committee's decision including a decision on validity or a decision under rule 69. Alternatively, the national authority may order that a hearing be reopened, or that a new hearing be held by the same or a different protest committee. When the national authority decides that there shall be a new hearing, it may appoint the protest committee.

**71.3**   When from the facts found by the protest committee the national authority decides that a boat that was a *party* to a protest hearing broke a *rule* and is not exonerated, it shall penalize her, whether or not that boat or that *rule* was mentioned in the protest committee's decision.

**71.4**   The decision of the national authority shall be final. The national authority shall send its decision in writing to all *parties* to the hearing and the protest committee, who shall be bound by the decision.

# PART 6
## ENTRY AND QUALIFICATION

**75**    **ENTERING A RACE**

**75.1**    To enter a race, a boat shall comply with the requirements of the organizing authority of the race. She shall be entered by

(a)    a member of a club or other organization affiliated to a World Sailing member national authority,

(b)    such a club or organization, or

(c)    a member of a World Sailing member national authority.

**75.2**    Competitors shall comply with World Sailing Regulation 19, Eligibility Code.

**76**    **EXCLUSION OF BOATS OR COMPETITORS**

**76.1**    The organizing authority or the race committee may reject or cancel the entry of a boat or exclude a competitor, subject to rule 76.3, provided it does so before the start of the first race and states the reason for doing so. On request the boat shall promptly be given the reason in writing. The boat may request redress if she considers that the rejection or exclusion is improper.

**76.2**    The organizing authority or the race committee shall not reject or cancel the entry of a boat or exclude a competitor because of advertising, provided the boat or competitor complies with World Sailing Regulation 20, Advertising Code.

**76.3**    At world and continental championships no entry within stated quotas shall be rejected or cancelled without first obtaining the approval of the relevant World Sailing Class Association (or the Offshore Racing Council) or World Sailing.

**77**    **IDENTIFICATION ON SAILS**

A boat shall comply with the requirements of Appendix G governing class insignia, national letters and numbers on sails.

**RYA** 78     **COMPLIANCE WITH CLASS RULES; CERTIFICATES**

78.1     While a boat is *racing*, her owner and any other person in charge shall ensure that the boat is maintained to comply with her class rules and that her measurement or rating certificate, if any, remains valid. In addition, the boat shall also comply at other times specified in the class rules, the notice of race or the sailing instructions.

78.2     When a *rule* requires a valid certificate to be produced or its existence verified before a boat *races*, and this cannot be done, the boat may *race* provided that the race committee receives a statement signed by the person in charge that a valid certificate exists. The boat shall produce the certificate or arrange for its existence to be verified by the race committee. The penalty for breaking this rule is disqualification without a hearing from all races of the event.

79     **CLASSIFICATION**

If the notice of race or class rules state that some or all competitors must satisfy classification requirements, the classification shall be carried out as described in World Sailing Regulation 22, Sailor Classification Code.

80     **ADVERTISING**

A boat and her crew shall comply with World Sailing Regulation 20, Advertising Code.

81     **RESCHEDULED EVENT**

When an event is rescheduled to dates different from the dates stated in the notice of race, all boats entered shall be notified. The race committee may accept new entries that meet all the entry requirements except the original deadline for entries.

# PART 7
## RACE ORGANIZATION

**84**   **GOVERNING RULES**

The organizing authority, race committee, technical committee, protest committee and other race officials shall be governed by the *rules* in the conduct and judging of races.

**85**   **CHANGES TO RULES**

**85.1**   A change to a *rule* shall refer specifically to the *rule* and state the change. A change to a *rule* includes an addition to it or deletion of all or part of it.

**85.2**   A change to one of the following types of *rules* may be made only as shown below.

| Type of rule | Change only if permitted by |
|---|---|
| Racing rule | Rule 86 |
| Rule in a World Sailing code | A rule in the code |
| National authority prescription | Rule 88.2 |
| Class rule | Rule 87 |
| Rule in the notice of race | Rule 89.2(b) |
| Rule in the sailing instructions | Rule 90.2(c) |
| Rule in any other document governing the event | A rule in the document itself |

**86**   **CHANGES TO THE RACING RULES**

**86.1**   A racing rule shall not be changed unless permitted in the rule itself or as follows:

(a)   Prescriptions of a national authority may change a racing rule, but not the Definitions; the Basic Principles; a rule in the Introduction; Part 1, 2 or 7; rule 42, 43, 63.4, 69, 70, 71, 75, 76.3, 79 or 80; a rule of an appendix that changes one of these rules; Appendix H or N; World Sailing Regulation 19, 20, 21, 22, 35 or 37.

(b)    The notice of race or sailing instructions may change a racing rule, but not rule 76.1 or 76.2, Appendix R, or a rule listed in rule 86.1(a).

(c)    Class rules may change only racing rules 42, 49, 50, 51, 52, 53 and 54.

**86.2**    In exception to rule 86.1, World Sailing may in limited circumstances (see World Sailing Regulation 28.1.3) authorize changes to the racing rules for a specific international event. The authorization shall be stated in a letter of approval to the event organizing authority and in the notice of race and sailing instructions, and the letter shall be posted on the event's official notice board.

**R⁄A 86.3**    If a national authority so prescribes, the restrictions in rule 86.1 do not apply if rules are changed to develop or test proposed rules. The national authority may prescribe that its approval is required for such changes.

## 87    CHANGES TO CLASS RULES

The notice of race or sailing instructions may change a class rule only when the class rules permit the change, or when written permission of the class association for the change is displayed on the official notice board.

## 88    NATIONAL PRESCRIPTIONS

### 88.1    Prescriptions that Apply

The prescriptions that apply to an event are the prescriptions of the national authority with which the organizing authority is associated under rule 89.1. However, if boats will pass through the waters of more than one national authority while *racing*, the notice of race or sailing instructions shall identify the prescriptions that will apply and when they will apply.

### R⁄A 88.2    Changes to Prescriptions

The notice of race or sailing instructions may change a prescription. However, a national authority may restrict changes to its prescriptions with a prescription to this rule, provided World Sailing approves its application to do so. The restricted prescriptions shall not be changed.

## 89      ORGANIZING AUTHORITY; NOTICE OF RACE; APPOINTMENT OF RACE OFFICIALS

### 89.1    Organizing Authority

Races shall be organized by an organizing authority, which shall be

(a)    World Sailing;

(b)    a member national authority of World Sailing;

(c)    an affiliated club;

(d)    an affiliated organization other than a club and, if so prescribed by the national authority, with the approval of the national authority or in conjunction with an affiliated club;

(e)    an unaffiliated class association, either with the approval of the national authority or in conjunction with an affiliated club;

(f)    two or more of the above organizations;

(g)    an unaffiliated body in conjunction with an affiliated club where the body is owned and controlled by the club. The national authority of the club may prescribe that its approval is required for such an event; or

(h)    if approved by World Sailing and the national authority of the club, an unaffiliated body in conjunction with an affiliated club where the body is not owned and controlled by the club.

In rule 89.1, an organization is affiliated if it is affiliated to the national authority of the venue; otherwise the organization is unaffiliated. However, if boats will pass through the waters of more than one national authority while *racing*, an organization is affiliated if it is affiliated to the national authority of one of the ports of call.

### 89.2    Notice of Race; Appointment of Race Officials

(a)    The organizing authority shall publish a notice of race that conforms to rule J1.

(b)    The notice of race may be changed provided adequate notice is given.

(c)    The organizing authority shall appoint a race committee and, when appropriate, appoint a protest committee, a technical committee and umpires. However, the race committee, an international jury, a technical committee and umpires may be appointed by World Sailing as provided in its regulations.

## 90    RACE COMMITTEE; SAILING INSTRUCTIONS; SCORING

### 90.1    Race Committee

The race committee shall conduct races as directed by the organizing authority and as required by the *rules*.

### 90.2    Sailing Instructions

(a)   The race committee shall publish written sailing instructions that conform to rule J2.

(b)   When appropriate, for an event where entries from other countries are expected, the sailing instructions shall include, in English, the applicable national prescriptions.

(c)   The sailing instructions may be changed provided the change is in writing and posted on the official notice board before the time stated in the sailing instructions or, on the water, communicated to each boat before her warning signal. Oral changes may be given only on the water, and only if the procedure is stated in the sailing instructions.

### 90.3    Scoring

(a)   The race committee shall score a race or series as provided in Appendix A using the Low Point System, unless the notice of race or sailing instructions specify some other system. A race shall be scored if it is not *abandoned* and if one boat sails the course in compliance with rule 28 and *finishes* within the time limit, if any, even if she retires after *finishing* or is disqualified.

(b)   When a scoring system provides for excluding one or more race scores, any score that is a Disqualification Not Excludable (DNE) shall be included in a boat's series score.

(c)   When the race committee determines from its own records or observations that it has scored a boat incorrectly, it shall correct the error and make the corrected scores available to competitors.

# 91    PROTEST COMMITTEE

A protest committee shall be

(a) a committee appointed by the organizing authority or race committee;

(b) an international jury appointed by the organizing authority or as prescribed in the World Sailing Regulations. It shall be composed as required by rule N1 and have the authority and responsibilities stated in rule N2. A national authority may prescribe that its approval is required for the appointment of international juries for races within its jurisdiction, except World Sailing events or when international juries are appointed by World Sailing under rule 89.2(c); or

(c) a committee appointed by the national authority under rule 71.2.

# 92    TECHNICAL COMMITTEE

**92.1** A technical committee shall be a committee of at least one member and be appointed by the organizing authority or the race committee or as prescribed in the World Sailing Regulations.

**92.2** The technical committee shall conduct equipment inspection and event measurement as directed by the organizing authority and as required by the *rules*.

# APPENDIX A
## SCORING

*See rule 90.3.*

**A1    NUMBER OF RACES**

The number of races scheduled and the number required to be completed to constitute a series shall be stated in the notice of race or sailing instructions.

**A2    SERIES SCORES**

**A2.1**    Each boat's series score shall, subject to rule 90.3(b), be the total of her race scores excluding her worst score. (The notice of race or sailing instructions may make a different arrangement by providing, for example, that no score will be excluded, that two or more scores will be excluded, or that a specified number of scores will be excluded if a specified number of races are completed. A race is completed if scored; see rule 90.3(a).) If a boat has two or more equal worst scores, the score(s) for the race(s) sailed earliest in the series shall be excluded. The boat with the lowest series score wins and others shall be ranked accordingly.

**A2.2**    If a boat has entered any race in a series, she shall be scored for the whole series.

**A3    STARTING TIMES AND FINISHING PLACES**

The time of a boat's starting signal shall be her starting time, and the order in which boats *finish* a race shall determine their finishing places. However, when a handicap or rating system is used a boat's corrected time shall determine her finishing place.

## A4     LOW POINT SYSTEM

*The Low Point System will apply unless the notice of race or sailing instructions specify another system; see rule 90.3(a).*

**A4.1**     Each boat *starting* and *finishing* and not thereafter retiring, being penalized or given redress shall be scored points as follows:

| Finishing place | Points |
|---|---|
| First | 1 |
| Second | 2 |
| Third | 3 |
| Fourth | 4 |
| Fifth | 5 |
| Sixth | 6 |
| Seventh | 7 |
| Each place thereafter | Add 1 point |

**A4.2**     A boat that did not *start*, did not *finish*, retired or was disqualified shall be scored points for the finishing place one more than the number of boats entered in the series. A boat that is penalized under rule 30.2 or that takes a penalty under rule 44.3(a) shall be scored points as provided in rule 44.3(c).

## A5     SCORES DETERMINED BY THE RACE COMMITTEE

A boat that did not *start* or *finish* or comply with rule 30.2, 30.3, 30.4 or 78.2, or that retires or takes a penalty under rule 44.3(a), shall be scored accordingly by the race committee without a hearing. Only the protest committee may take other scoring actions that worsen a boat's score.

## A6     CHANGES IN PLACES AND SCORES OF OTHER BOATS

**A6.1**     If a boat is disqualified from a race or retires after *finishing*, each boat with a worse finishing place shall be moved up one place.

**A6.2**     If the protest committee decides to give redress by adjusting a boat's score, the scores of other boats shall not be changed unless the protest committee decides otherwise.

## A7     RACE TIES

If boats are tied at the finishing line or if a handicap or rating system is used and boats have equal corrected times, the points for the place for which the boats have tied and for the place(s) immediately below shall be added together and divided equally. Boats tied for a race prize shall share it or be given equal prizes.

## A8     SERIES TIES

**A8.1**     If there is a series-score tie between two or more boats, each boat's race scores shall be listed in order of best to worst, and at the first point(s) where there is a difference the tie shall be broken in favour of the boat(s) with the best score(s). No excluded scores shall be used.

**A8.2**     If a tie remains between two or more boats, they shall be ranked in order of their scores in the last race. Any remaining ties shall be broken by using the tied boats' scores in the next-to-last race and so on until all ties are broken. These scores shall be used even if some of them are excluded scores.

## A9     RACE SCORES IN A SERIES LONGER THAN A REGATTA

For a series that is held over a period of time longer than a regatta, a boat that came to the starting area but did not *start*, did not *finish*, retired or was disqualified shall be scored points for the finishing place one more than the number of boats that came to the starting area. A boat that did not come to the starting area shall be scored points for the finishing place one more than the number of boats entered in the series.

## A10     GUIDANCE ON REDRESS

If the protest committee decides to give redress by adjusting a boat's score for a race, it is advised to consider scoring her

(a)     points equal to the average, to the nearest tenth of a point (0.05 to be rounded upward), of her points in all the races in the series except the race in question;

(b)     points equal to the average, to the nearest tenth of a point (0.05 to be rounded upward), of her points in all the races before the race in question; or

(c)     points based on the position of the boat in the race at the time of the incident that justified redress.

**A11**    **SCORING ABBREVIATIONS**

These scoring abbreviations shall be used for recording the circumstances described:

DNC    Did not *start*; did not come to the starting area

DNS    Did not *start* (other than DNC and OCS)

OCS    Did not *start*; on the course side of the starting line at her starting signal and failed to *start*, or broke rule 30.1

ZFP    20% penalty under rule 30.2

UFD    Disqualification under rule 30.3

BFD    Disqualification under rule 30.4

SCP    Scoring Penalty applied

DNF    Did not *finish*

RET    Retired

DSQ    Disqualification

DNE    Disqualification that is not excludable

RDG    Redress given

DPI    Discretionary penalty imposed

# APPENDIX B
# WINDSURFING COMPETITION RULES

*Windsurfing races shall be sailed under* The Racing Rules of Sailing *as changed by this appendix. The term 'boat' elsewhere in the racing rules means 'board' or 'boat' as appropriate. The term 'heat' means one elimination race, a 'round' consists of several heats, and an 'elimination series' consists of one or more rounds. However, in speed competition, a 'round' consists of one or more speed 'runs'.*

*A windsurfing event can include one or more of the following disciplines or their formats:*

| Discipline | Formats |
|---|---|
| Racing | Course racing; Slalom; Marathon |
| Expression | Wave performance; Freestyle |
| Speed | Standard Offshore Speed Course; Speed Crossings; Alpha Speed Course |

*In racing or expression competition, boards may compete in elimination series, and only a limited number of them may advance from round to round. A marathon race is a race scheduled to last more than one hour.*

*In expression competition a board's performance is judged on skill and variety rather than speed and is organized using elimination series. Either wave performance or freestyle competition is organized, depending on the wave conditions at the venue.*

*In speed competition a board's performance is based on her speed over a measured course. Boards take turns sailing runs over the course.*

## CHANGES TO THE DEFINITIONS

The definitions *Mark-Room*, and *Tack, Starboard* or *Port* are deleted and replaced by:

***Mark-Room*** *Mark-Room* for a board is *room* to sail her *proper course* to round or pass the *mark*. However, *mark-room* for a board does not include *room* to tack unless she is *overlapped* inside and to *windward* of the board required to give *mark-room* and she would be *fetching* the *mark* after her tack.

**Tack, Starboard or Port**   A board is on the *tack*, *starboard* or *port*, corresponding to the competitor's hand that would be nearer the mast if the competitor were in normal sailing position with both hands on the wishbone and arms not crossed. A board is on *starboard tack* when the competitor's right hand would be nearer the mast and is on *port tack* when the competitor's left hand would be nearer the mast.

The definition *Zone* is deleted.

Add the following definitions:

**Capsized**   A board is *capsized* when she is not under control because her sail or the competitor is in the water.

**Rounding or Passing**   A board is *rounding or passing* a *mark* from the time her *proper course* is to begin to manoeuvre to round or pass it, until the *mark* has been rounded or passed.

## B1     CHANGES TO THE RULES OF PART 1

*[No changes.]*

## B2     CHANGES TO THE RULES OF PART 2

### B2.13   WHILE TACKING

Rule 13 is changed to:

After a board passes head to wind, she shall *keep clear* of other boards until her sail has filled. During that time rules 10, 11 and 12 do not apply. If two boards are subject to this rule at the same time, the one on the other's port side or the one astern shall *keep clear*.

**B2.17**    Rule 17 is deleted and replaced by

### ON THE SAME TACK BEFORE A REACHING START

When, at the warning signal, the course to the first *mark* is approximately ninety degrees from the true wind, a board *overlapped* to *leeward* of another board on the same *tack* during the last 30 seconds before her starting signal shall not sail above the shortest course to the first *mark* while they remain *overlapped* if as a result the other board would need to take action to avoid contact, unless in doing so she promptly sails astern of the other board.

### B2.18  MARK-ROOM

Rule 18 is changed as follows:

The first sentence of rule 18.1 is changed to:

Rule B2.18 applies between boards when they are required to leave a *mark* on the same side and at least one of them is *rounding or passing* it.

Rule 18.2(b) is changed to:

(b)    If boards are *overlapped* when the first of them is *rounding or passing* the *mark*, the outside board at that moment shall thereafter give the inside board *mark-room*. If a board is *clear ahead* when she is *rounding or passing* the *mark*, the board *clear astern* at that moment shall thereafter give her *mark-room*.

Rule 18.2(c) is changed to:

(c)    When a board is required to give *mark-room* by rule B2.18.2(b), she shall continue to do so even if later an *overlap* is broken or a new *overlap* begins. However, if the board entitled to *mark-room* passes head to wind, rule B2.18.2(b) ceases to apply.

### B2.18.4  Gybing or Bearing Away

Rule 18.4 is changed to:

When an inside *overlapped* right-of-way board must gybe or bear away at a *mark* to sail her *proper course*, until she gybes or bears away she shall sail no farther from the *mark* than needed to sail that course. Rule B2.18.4 does not apply at a gate *mark*.

### B2.23    CAPSIZED; AGROUND; RESCUING

Rule 23 is changed to:

**B2.23.1** If possible, a board shall avoid a board that is *capsized* or has not regained control after *capsizing*, is aground, or is trying to help a person or vessel in danger.

**B2.23.2** If possible, a board that is *capsized* or aground shall not interfere with another board.

### B2.24    INTERFERING WITH ANOTHER BOARD; SAIL OUT OF WATER

Add new rule B2.24.3:

**B2.24.3** In the last minute before her starting signal, a board shall have her sail out of the water and in a normal position, except when accidentally *capsized*.

### PART 2 RULES DELETED

Rule 18.3 is deleted.

### B3    CHANGES TO THE RULES OF PART 3

### B3.26    STARTING RACES

Rule 26 is changed to:

### B3.26.1  System 1

Races shall be started by using the following signals. Times shall be taken from the visual signals; the absence of a sound signal shall be disregarded.

| Minutes before starting signal | Visual signal | Sound signal | Means |
|---|---|---|---|
| 5* | Class flag | One | Warning signal |
| 4 | P, I, Z, Z with I, U, or black flag | One | Preparatory signal |
| 1 | Preparatory flag removed | One long | One minute |
| 0 | Class flag removed | One | Starting signal |

*or as stated in the sailing instructions

The warning signal for each succeeding class shall be made with or after the starting signal of the preceding class.

### B3.26.2  System 2

Races shall be started by using the following signals. Times shall be taken from the visual signals; the absence of a sound signal shall be disregarded.

| Minutes before starting signal | Visual signal | Sound signal | Means |
|---|---|---|---|
| 3 | Class flag or heat number | | Attention signal |
| 2 | Red flag; attention signal removed | One | Warning signal |
| 1 | Yellow flag; red flag removed | One | Preparatory signal |
| $\frac{1}{2}$ | Yellow flag removed | | 30 seconds |
| 0 | Green flag | One | Starting signal |

### B3.26.3  System 3 (for Beach Starts)

(a)    When the starting line is on the beach, or so close to the beach that the competitor must stand in the water to *start*, the start is a beach start.

(b)    The starting stations shall be numbered so that station 1 is the most windward one. Unless the sailing instructions specify some other system, a board's starting station shall be determined

    (1)    for the first race or round of the event, by draw, or

    (2)    for any race or round after the first one, by her place in the previous race or heat (The first place on station 1, the second place on station 2, and so on).

(c)    After boards have been called to take their positions, the race committee shall make the preparatory signal by displaying a red flag with one sound. The starting signal shall be made, at any time after the preparatory signal, by removing the red flag with one sound.

(d)    After the starting signal each board shall take the shortest route from her starting station to the water and then to her sailing position without interfering with other boards. Part 2 rules will apply when both of the competitor's feet are on the board.

### B3.31   TOUCHING A MARK

Rule 31 is changed to:

A board may touch a *mark* but shall not hold on to it.

## B4        CHANGES TO THE RULES OF PART 4

### B4.42   PROPULSION

Rule 42 is changed to:

A board shall be propelled only by the action of the wind on the sail, by the action of the water on the hull and by the unassisted actions of the competitor. However, significant progress shall not be made by paddling, swimming or walking.

### B4.43   COMPETITOR CLOTHING AND EQUIPMENT

Rule 43.1(a) is changed to:

(a)    Competitors shall not wear or carry clothing or equipment for the purpose of increasing their weight. However, a competitor may wear a drinking container that shall have a capacity of at least one litre and weigh no more than 1.5 kilograms when full.

### B4.44   PENALTIES AT THE TIME OF AN INCIDENT

Rule 44 is changed to:

### B4.44.1   Taking a Penalty

A board may take a 360°-Turn Penalty when she may have broken one of more rules of Part 2 in an incident while *racing*. The sailing instructions may specify the use of some other penalty. However, if the board caused injury or serious damage or, despite taking a penalty, gained a significant advantage in the race or series by her breach, her penalty shall be to retire.

### B4.44.2   360°-Turn Penalty

After getting well clear of other boards as soon after the incident as possible, a board takes a 360°-Turn Penalty by promptly making a 360° turn with no requirement for a tack or a gybe. When a board takes the penalty at or near the finishing line, she shall sail completely to the course side of the line before *finishing*.

### PART 4 RULES DELETED

Rules 43.2, 44.3, 45, 47.2, 48.1, 49, 50, 51, 52 and 54 are deleted.

## B5      CHANGES TO THE RULES OF PART 5

### B5.60      RIGHT TO PROTEST; RIGHT TO REQUEST REDRESS OR RULE 69 ACTION

Rule 60.1(a) is changed by deleting 'or saw'.

### B5.61   PROTEST REQUIREMENTS

The first three sentences of rule 61.1(a) are changed to:

A board intending to protest shall inform the other board at the first reasonable opportunity. When her *protest* will concern an incident in the racing area that she was involved in or saw, she shall hail 'Protest'. She shall also inform the race committee of her intention to protest as soon as practicable after she *finishes* or retires.

### B5.62  REDRESS

Rule 62.1(b) is changed to:

(b)   injury, physical damage or *capsize* because of the action of

    (1)   a board that broke a rule of Part 2 and took the appropriate penalty or was penalized, or

    (2)   a vessel not *racing* that was required to keep clear.

### B5.64  DECISIONS

Rule 64.3(b) is changed to:

(b)   When the protest committee is in doubt about a matter concerning the measurement of a board, the meaning of a class rule, or damage to a board, it shall refer its questions, together with the relevant facts, to an authority responsible for interpreting the rule. In making its decision, the committee shall be bound by the reply of the authority.

## B6    CHANGES TO THE RULES OF PART 6

### B6.78  COMPLIANCE WITH CLASS RULES; CERTIFICATES

Add to rule 78.1: 'When so prescribed by World Sailing, a numbered and dated device on a board and her centreboard, fin and rig shall serve as her measurement certificate.'

## B7    CHANGES TO THE RULES OF PART 7

### B7.90  RACE COMMITTEE; SAILING INSTRUCTIONS; SCORING

The last sentence of rule 90.2(c) is changed to: 'Oral instructions may be given only if the procedure is stated in the sailing instructions.'

## B8    CHANGES TO APPENDIX A

### B8.A1  NUMBER OF RACES; OVERALL SCORES

Rule A1 is changed to:

The number of races scheduled and the number required to be completed to constitute a series shall be stated in the notice of race or sailing instructions. If an event includes more than one discipline or format, the notice of race or sailing instructions shall state how the overall scores are to be calculated.

### B8.A2.1  SERIES SCORES

Rule A2.1 is changed to:

Each board's series score shall, subject to rule 90.3(b), be the total of her race scores excluding her

(a)   worst score when from 5 to 11 races have been completed, or

(b)   two worst scores when 12 or more races have been completed.

(The notice of race or sailing instructions may make a different arrangement. A race is completed if scored; see rule 90.3(a).) If a board has two or more equal worst scores, the score(s) for the race(s) sailed earliest in the series shall be excluded. The board with the lowest series score wins and others shall be ranked accordingly.

### B8.A8  SERIES TIES

Rule A8 is changed to:

**B8.A8.1**   If there is a series-score tie between two or more boards, they shall be ranked in order of their best excluded race score.

**B8.A8.2**   If a tie remains between two or more boards, each board's race scores, including excluded scores, shall be listed in order of best to worst, and at the first point(s) where there is a difference the tie shall be broken in favour of the board(s) with the best score(s). These scores shall be used even if some of them are excluded scores.

**B8.A8.3**   If a tie still remains between two or more boards, they shall be ranked in order of their scores in the last race. Any remaining ties shall be broken by using the tied boards' scores in the next-to-last race and so on until all ties are broken. These scores shall be used even if some of them are excluded scores.

**B9     CHANGES TO APPENDIX G**

**B9.G1   WORLD SAILING CLASS BOARDS**

**B9.G1.3   Positioning**

Rule G1.3(a) is changed to:

(a)     The class insignia shall be displayed once on each side of the sail in the area above a line projected at right angles from a point on the luff of the sail one-third of the distance from the head to the wishbone. The national letters and sail numbers shall be in the central third of that part of the sail above the wishbone, clearly separated from any advertising. They shall be black and applied back to back on an opaque white background. The background shall extend a minimum of 30 mm beyond the characters. There shall be a '–' between the national letters and the sail number, and the spacing between characters shall be adequate for legibility.

**APPENDIX G RULES DELETED**

The first sentence of rule G1.3(b) is deleted. Rules G1.3(c), G1.3(d) and G1.3(e) are deleted.

**B10     CHANGES TO RULES FOR EVENTS THAT INCLUDE ELIMINATION SERIES**

**B10.29   RECALLS**

For a race of an elimination series that will qualify a board to compete in a later stage of an event, rule 29 is changed to:

(a)     When at a board's starting signal any part of her hull, crew or equipment is on the course side of the starting line, the race committee shall signal a general recall.

(b)     If the race committee acts under rule B10.29(a) and the board is identified, she shall be disqualified without a hearing, even if the race is *abandoned*. The race committee shall hail or display her sail number, and she shall leave the course area immediately. If the race is restarted or resailed, she shall not sail in it.

(c)     If the race was completed but was later *abandoned* by the protest committee, and if the race is resailed, a board disqualified under rule B10.29(b) may sail in it.

## B10.37    ELIMINATION SERIES INCLUDING HEATS

Add new rule B10.37:

*Rule B10.37 applies in elimination series in which boards compete in heats.*

### B10.37.1    Elimination Series Procedure

(a) Competition shall take the form of one or more elimination series. Each of them shall consist of either rounds in a single elimination series where only a number of the best scorers advance, or rounds in a double elimination series where boards have more than one opportunity to advance.

(b) Boards shall sail one against another in pairs, or in groups determined by the elimination ladder. The selected form of competition shall not be changed while a round remains uncompleted.

### B10.37.2    Seeding and Ranking Lists

(a) When a seeding or ranking list is used to establish the heats of the first round, places 1–8 (four heats) or 1–16 (eight heats) shall be distributed evenly among the heats.

(b) For a subsequent elimination series, if any, boards shall be reassigned to new heats according to the ranking in the previous elimination series.

(c) The organizing authority's seeding decisions are final and are not grounds for a request for redress.

### B10.37.3    Heat Schedule

The schedule of heats shall be posted on the official notice board no later than 30 minutes before the starting signal for the first heat.

### B10.37.4    Advancement and Byes

(a) In racing and expression competition, the boards in each heat to advance to the next round shall be announced by the race committee no later than 10 minutes before the starting signal for the first heat. The number advancing may be changed by the protest committee as a result of a redress decision.

(b) In expression competition, any first-round byes shall be assigned to the highest-seeded boards.

(c) In wave performance competition, only the winner of each heat shall advance to the next round.

(d) In freestyle competition, boards shall advance to the next round as follows: from an eight-board heat, the best four advance, and the winner will sail against the fourth and the second against the third; from a four-board heat, the best two advance and will sail against each other.

## B10.37.5 Finals

(a) The final shall consist of a maximum of three races. The race committee shall announce the number of races to be sailed in the final no later than 5 minutes before the warning signal for the first final race.

(b) A runners-up final may be sailed after the final. All boards in the semi-final heats that failed to qualify for the final may compete in it.

## B10.63    HEARINGS

For a race of an elimination series that will qualify a board to compete in a later stage of an event, rules 61.2 and 65.2 are deleted and rule 63.6 is changed to:

## B10.63.6  Taking Evidence and Finding Facts

*Protests* and requests for redress need not be in writing; they shall be made orally to a member of the protest committee as soon as reasonably possible following the race. The protest committee may take evidence in any way it considers appropriate and may communicate its decision orally.

## B10.70    APPEALS AND REQUESTS TO A NATIONAL AUTHORITY

Add new rule B10.70.7:

## B10.70.7  Appeals are not permitted in disciplines and formats with elimination series.

### B10.A2.1  SERIES SCORES

Rule A2.1 is changed to:

Each board's elimination series score shall, subject to rule 90.3(b), be the total of her race scores excluding her

(a)    worst score when 3 or 4 races are completed,

(b)    two worst scores when from 5 to 7 races are completed,

(c)    three worst scores when 8 or more races are completed.

Each board's final series score shall be the total of her race scores excluding her worst score when 3 races are completed. (The notice of race or sailing instructions may make a different arrangement. A race is completed if scored; see rule 90.3(a).) If a board has two or more equal worst scores, the score(s) for the race(s) sailed earliest in the series shall be excluded. The board with the lowest series score wins and others shall be ranked accordingly.

### B10.A4  LOW POINT SYSTEM

Add at the end of the first sentence of rule A4.2: 'or, in a race of an elimination series, the number of boards in that heat'.

Add new rule B10.A4.3:

**B10.A4.3**    When a heat cannot be completed, the points for the unscored places shall be added together and divided by the number of places in that heat. The resulting number of points, to the nearest tenth of a point (0.05 to be rounded upward), shall be given to each board entered in the heat.

## B11    CHANGES TO RULES FOR EXPRESSION COMPETITION

Add the following definitions:

***Coming In*** and ***Going Out***   A board sailing in the same direction as the incoming surf is *coming in*. A board sailing in the direction opposite to the incoming surf is *going out*.

***Jumping***    A board is *jumping* when she takes off at the top of a wave while *going out*.

***Overtaking***    A board is *overtaking* from the moment she gains an *overlap* from *clear astern* until the moment she is *clear ahead* of the *overtaken* board.

**Possession**   The first board sailing shoreward immediately in front of a wave has *possession* of that wave. However, when it is impossible to determine which board is first the *windward* board has possession.

**Recovering**   A board is *recovering* from the time her sail or, when water-starting, the competitor is out of the water until she has steerage way.

**Surfing**   A board is *surfing* when she is on or immediately in front of a wave while *coming in*.

**Transition**   A board changing *tacks*, or taking off while *coming in*, or one that is not *surfing*, *jumping*, *capsized* or *recovering* is in *transition*.

### B11. PART 2 – WHEN BOARDS MEET

The rules of Part 2 are deleted and replaced by:

(a)   COMING IN AND GOING OUT

A board *coming in* shall *keep clear* of a board *going out*. When two boards are *going out* or *coming in* while on the same wave, or when neither is *going out* or *coming in*, a board on *port tack* shall *keep clear* of the one on *starboard tack*.

(b)   BOARDS ON THE SAME WAVE, COMING IN

When two or more boards are on a wave *coming in*, a board that does not have *possession* shall *keep clear*.

(c)   CLEAR ASTERN, CLEAR AHEAD AND OVERTAKING

A board *clear astern* and not on a wave shall *keep clear* of a board *clear ahead*. An *overtaking* board that is not on a wave shall *keep clear*.

(d)   TRANSITION

A board in *transition* shall *keep clear* of one that is not. When two boards are in *transition* at the same time, the one on the other's port side or the one astern shall *keep clear*.

(e)   JUMPING

A board that is *jumping* shall *keep clear* of one that is not.

## B11.26  STARTING AND ENDING HEATS

Rule 26 is changed to:

Heats shall be started and ended by using the following signals:

(a)  STARTING A HEAT

Each flag shall be removed when the next flag is displayed.

| Minutes before starting signal | Visual signal | Sound signal | Means |
|---|---|---|---|
| Beginning of transition period | Heat number with red flag | One | Warning |
| 1 | Yellow flag | One | Preparatory |
| 0 | Green flag | One | Starting signal |

(b)  ENDING A HEAT

| Minutes before starting signal | Visual signal | Sound signal | Means |
|---|---|---|---|
| 1 | Green flag removed | One | End warning |
| 0 | Red flag | One | Ending signal |

## B11.38  REGISTRATION; COURSE AREA; HEAT DURATION; ADVANCEMENT AND BYES

Add new rule B11.38:

(a)  Boards shall register with the race committee the colours and other particulars of their sails, or their identification according to another method stated in the sailing instructions, no later than the starting signal for the heat two heats before their own.

(b)  The course area shall be defined in the sailing instructions and posted on the official notice board no later than 10 minutes before the starting signal for the first heat. A board shall be scored only while sailing in the course area.

(c)   Any change in heat duration shall be announced by the race committee no later than 15 minutes before the starting signal for the first heat in the next round.

(d)   Rule B10.37.4 applies.

## B11.41   OUTSIDE HELP

Change the number of rule 41 to B11.41.1 and add new rule B11.41.2:

## B11.41.2

An assistant may provide replacement equipment to a board. The assistant shall not interfere with other competing boards. A board whose assistant interferes with another board may be penalized at the discretion of the protest committee.

## APPENDIX A – SCORING

The rules of Appendix A are deleted and replaced by:

## B11.A1   EXPRESSION COMPETITON SCORING

(a)   Expression competition shall be scored by a panel of three judges. However, the panel may have a greater odd number of members, and there may be two such panels. Each judge shall give points for each manoeuvre based on the scale stated in the notice of race or sailing instructions.

(b)   The criteria of scoring shall be decided by the race committee and announced on the official notice board no later than 30 minutes before the starting signal for the first heat.

(c)   A board's heat standing shall be determined by adding together the points given by each judge. The board with the highest score wins and others shall be ranked accordingly.

(d)   Both semi-final heats shall have been sailed for an elimination series to be valid.

(e)   Except for members of the race committee responsible for scoring the event, only competitors in the heat shall be allowed to see judges' score sheets for the heat. Each score sheet shall bear the full name of the judge.

(f)   Scoring decisions of the judges shall not be grounds for a request for redress by a board.

### B11.A2  SERIES TIES

(a) In a heat, if there is a tie in the total points given by one or more judges, it shall be broken in favour of the board with the higher single score in the priority category. If the categories are weighted equally, in wave performance competition the tie shall be broken in favour of the board with the higher single score in wave riding, and in freestyle competition in favour of the board with the higher score for overall impression. If a tie remains, in wave performance competition it shall be broken in favour of the board with the higher single score in the category without priority, and in freestyle competition it shall stand as the final result.

(b) If there is a tie in the series score, it shall be broken in favour of the board that scored better more times than the other board. All scores shall be used even if some of them are excluded scores.

(c) If a tie still remains, the heat shall be resailed. If this is not possible, the tie shall stand as the final result.

## B12    CHANGES TO RULES FOR SPEED COMPETITION

The rules of Part 2 are deleted and replaced by:

### B12.PART 2 – GENERAL RULES

(a) WATER STARTING

A board shall not water start on the course or in the starting area, except to sail off the course to avoid boards that are making, or about to make, a run.

(b) LEAVING THE COURSE AREA

A board leaving the course area shall *keep clear* of boards making a run.

(c) COURSE CONTROL

When the race committee points an orange flag at a board, she is penalized and the run shall not be counted.

(d)    RETURNING TO THE STARTING AREA

A board returning to the starting area shall keep clear of the course.

(e)    MAXIMUM NUMBER OF RUNS FOR EACH BOARD

The maximum number of runs that may be made by each board in a round shall be announced by the race committee no later than 15 minutes before the starting signal for the first round.

(f)    DURATION OF A ROUND

The duration of a round shall be announced by the race committee no later than 15 minutes before the starting signal for the next round.

(g)    CONDITIONS FOR ESTABLISHING A RECORD

The minimum distance for a world record is 500 metres. Other records may be established over shorter distances. The course shall be defined by posts and transits ashore or by buoys afloat. Transits shall not converge.

(h)    VERIFICATION RULES

(1)    An observer appointed by the World Sailing Speed Record Council shall be present and verify run times and speeds at world record attempts. The race committee shall verify run times and speeds at other record attempts.

(2)    A competitor shall not enter the timing control area or discuss any timing matter directly with the timing organization. Any timing question shall be directed to the race committee.

## B12.26    STARTING AND ENDING A ROUND

Rule 26 is changed to:

Rounds shall be started and ended by using the following signals. Each flag shall be removed when the next flag is displayed.

(a)    STARTING A ROUND

| Signal | Flag | Means |
|---|---|---|
| Stand-by | AP flag | Course closed. Races are *postponed* |
| Course closed | Red flag | Course closed; will open shortly |
| Preparatory | Red and yellow flag | Course will open in 5 minutes |
| Starting | Green flag | Course is open |

(b)    ENDING A ROUND

| Signal | Flag | Means |
|---|---|---|
| End warning | Green and yellow flag | Course will be closed in 5 minutes |
| Extension | Yellow flag | Current round extended by 15 minutes |
| Round ended | Red flag | A new round will be started shortly |

## B12.64  DECISIONS

Rule 64.1 is deleted and replaced by:

### B12.64.1  Penalties

(a)    If a board fails to comply with a rule, she may be warned. If a board is warned a second time during the same round, she shall be excluded by the race committee from the remainder of the round. A list of the sail numbers of boards that have received warnings or have been excluded shall be posted on a notice board near the finishing line.

(b)    A board observed in the course area after having been excluded from a round shall be excluded from the competition without a hearing, and none of her previous times or results shall be valid.

(c)    Any breach of the verification rules may result in exclusion from one or more rounds or from the competition.

## APPENDIX A – SCORING

The rules of Appendix A are deleted and replaced by:

### B12.A1  SPEED COMPETITON SCORING

(a) On Standard Offshore Speed Courses, the speeds of a board's fastest two runs in a round shall be averaged to determine her standing in that round. The board with the highest average wins and others shall be ranked accordingly. If boards are tied, the tie shall be broken in favour of the board with the fastest run in the round.

(b) On Speed Crossings and Alpha Speed Courses, boards shall be ranked based on their fastest run in the round.

(c) If there is a series-score tie between two or more boards, it shall be broken in favour of the board(s) with the fastest run during the competition. If a tie remains, it shall be broken by applying rules B8.A8.2 and B8.A8.3.

# APPENDIX C
## MATCH RACING RULES

*Match races shall be sailed under* The Racing Rules of Sailing *as changed by this appendix. Matches shall be umpired unless the notice of race and sailing instructions state otherwise.*

*Note: A Standard Notice of Race, Standard Sailing Instructions, and Match Racing Rules for Blind Competitors are available at the World Sailing website.*

**C1**    **TERMINOLOGY**

'Competitor' means the skipper, team or boat as appropriate for the event. 'Flight' means two or more matches started in the same starting sequence.

**C2**    **CHANGES TO THE DEFINITIONS AND THE RULES OF PARTS 1, 2, 3 AND 4**

**C2.1**    The definition *Finish* is changed to:

> **Finish**    A boat *finishes* when any part of her hull crosses the finishing line in the direction of the course from the last *mark* after completing any penalties. However, when penalties are cancelled under rule C7.2(d) after one or both boats have *finished* each shall be recorded as *finished* when she crossed the line.

**C2.2**    The definition *Mark-Room* is changed to:

> **Mark-Room**    *Room* for a boat to sail her *proper course* to round or pass the *mark* on the required side.

**C2.3**    Add to the definition *Proper Course*: 'A boat taking a penalty or manoeuvring to take a penalty is not sailing a *proper course*.'

**C2.4**    In the definition *Zone* the distance is changed to two hull lengths.

**C2.5**     Add new rule 8 to Part 1:

## 8     LAST POINT OF CERTAINTY

The umpires will assume that the state of a boat, or her relationship to another boat, has not changed, until they are certain that it has changed.

**C2.6**     Rule 13 is changed to:

## 13     WHILE TACKING OR GYBING

**13.1**     After a boat passes head to wind, she shall *keep clear* of other boats until she is on a close-hauled course.

**13.2**     After the foot of the mainsail of a boat sailing downwind crosses the centreline she shall *keep clear* of other boats until her mainsail has filled or she is no longer sailing downwind.

**13.3**     While rule 13.1 or 13.2 applies, rules 10, 11 and 12 do not. However, if two boats are subject to rule 13.1 or 13.2 at the same time, the one on the other's port side or the one astern shall *keep clear*.

**C2.7**     Rule 16.2 is deleted.

**C2.8**     Rule 17 is deleted.

**C2.9**     Rule 18 is changed to:

## 18     MARK-ROOM

### 18.1     When Rule 18 Applies

Rule 18 applies between boats when they are required to leave a *mark* on the same side and at least one of them is in the *zone*. However, it does not apply between a boat approaching a *mark* and one leaving it.

### 18.2     Giving Mark-Room

(a) When the first boat reaches the *zone*,

   (1) if boats are *overlapped*, the outside boat at that moment shall thereafter give the inside boat *mark-room*.

   (2) if boats are not *overlapped*, the boat that has not reached the *zone* shall thereafter give *mark-room*.

(b) If the boat entitled to *mark-room* leaves the *zone*, the entitlement to *mark-room* ceases and rule 18.2(a) is applied again if required based on the relationship of the boats at the time rule 18.2(a) is re-applied.

(c) If a boat obtained an inside *overlap* and, from the time the *overlap* began, the outside boat is unable to give *mark-room*, she is not required to give it.

## 18.3    Tacking or Gybing

(a) If *mark-room* for a boat includes a change of *tack*, such tack or gybe shall be done no faster than a tack or gybe to sail her *proper course*.

(b) When an inside *overlapped* right-of-way boat must change *tack* at a *mark* to sail her *proper course*, until she changes *tack* she shall sail no farther from the *mark* than needed to sail that course. Rule 18.3(b) does not apply at a gate *mark* or a finishing *mark* and a boat shall not be penalized for breaking this rule unless the course of another boat was affected by the breach of this rule.

**C2.10**    When rule 20 applies, the following arm signals by the helmsman are required in addition to the hails:

(a) for 'Room to tack', repeatedly and clearly pointing to windward; and

(b) for 'You tack', repeatedly and clearly pointing at the other boat and waving the arm to windward.

**C2.11**    Rule 22.3 is deleted.

**C2.12**    Rule 24.1 is changed to: 'If reasonably possible, a boat not *racing* shall not interfere with a boat that is *racing* or an umpire boat.'

**C2.13**    Add new rule 24.3: 'When boats in different matches meet, any change of course by either boat shall be consistent with complying with a *rule* or trying to win her own match.'

**C2.14**    Rule 31 is changed to:

### 31    TOUCHING A MARK

While *racing*, neither the crew nor any part of a boat's hull shall touch a starting *mark* before *starting*, a *mark* that begins, bounds or ends the leg of the course on which she is sailing, or a finishing *mark* after *finishing*. In addition, while *racing*, a boat shall not touch a race committee vessel that is also a *mark*.

**C2.15**    Rule 42 shall also apply between the warning and preparatory signals.

**C2.16**    Rule 42.2(d) is changed to: 'sculling: repeated movement of the helm to propel the boat forward;'.

## C3    RACE SIGNALS AND CHANGES TO RELATED RULES

### C3.1    Starting Signals

The signals for starting a match shall be as follows. Times shall be taken from the visual signals; the failure of a sound signal shall be disregarded. If more than one match will be sailed, the starting signal for one match shall be the warning signal for the next match.

| Time in minutes | Visual signal | Sound signal | Means |
|---|---|---|---|
| 10 | Flag F displayed | One | Attention signal |
| 6 | Flag F removed | None | |
| 5 | Numeral pennant displayed* | One | Warning signal |
| 4 | Flag P displayed | One | Preparatory signal |
| 2 | Blue or yellow flag or both displayed** | One** | End of pre-start entry time |
| 1 | Flag P removed | One long | |
| 0 | Warning signal removed | One | Starting signal |

\* Within a flight, numeral pennant 1 means Match 1, pennant 2 means Match 2, etc., unless the sailing instructions state otherwise.

\*\* These signals shall be made only if one or both boats fail to comply with rule C4.2. The flag(s) shall be displayed until the umpires have signalled a penalty or for one minute, whichever is earlier.

### C3.2    Changes to Related Rules

(a)    Rule 29.1 is changed to:

(1)    When at a boat's starting signal any part of her hull, crew or equipment is on the course side of the starting line or one of its extensions, the race committee shall promptly display a blue or yellow flag identifying the boat with

one sound. The flag shall be displayed until the boat is completely on the pre-start side of the starting line or one of its extensions or until two minutes after her starting signal, whichever is earlier.

(2)   When after her starting signal a boat sails from the pre-start side to the course side of the starting line across an extension without having *started* correctly, the race committee shall promptly display a blue or yellow flag identifying the boat. The flag shall be displayed until the boat is completely on the pre-start side of the starting line or one of its extensions or until two minutes after her starting signal, whichever is earlier.

(b)   In the race signal AP the last sentence is changed to: 'The attention signal will be made 1 minute after removal unless at that time the race is *postponed* again or *abandoned*.'

(c)   In the race signal N the last sentence is changed to: 'The attention signal will be made 1 minute after removal unless at that time the race is *abandoned* again or *postponed*.'

**C3.3     Finishing Line Signals**

The race signal Blue flag or shape shall not be used.

**C4          REQUIREMENTS BEFORE THE START**

**C4.1**     At her preparatory signal, each boat shall be outside the line that is at a 90° angle to the starting line through the starting *mark* at her assigned end. In the pairing list, the boat listed on the left-hand side is assigned the port end and shall display a blue flag at her stern while *racing*. The other boat is assigned the starboard end and shall display a yellow flag at her stern while *racing*.

**C4.2**     Within the two-minute period following her preparatory signal, a boat shall cross and clear the starting line, the first time from the course side to the pre-start side.

**C5          SIGNALS BY UMPIRES**

**C5.1**     A green and white flag with one long sound means 'No penalty'.

**C5.2**     A blue or yellow flag identifying a boat with one long sound means 'The identified boat shall take a penalty by complying with rule C7.'

**C5.3**  A red flag with or soon after a blue or yellow flag with one long sound means 'The identified boat shall take a penalty by complying with rule C7.3(d).'

**C5.4**  A black flag with a blue or yellow flag and one long sound means 'The identified boat is disqualified, and the match is terminated and awarded to the other boat.'

**C5.5**  One short sound means 'A penalty is now completed.'

**C5.6**  Repetitive short sounds mean 'A boat is no longer taking a penalty and the penalty remains.'

**C5.7**  A blue or yellow flag or shape displayed from an umpire boat means 'The identified boat has an outstanding penalty.'

## C6    PROTESTS AND REQUESTS FOR REDRESS BY BOATS

**C6.1**  A boat may protest another boat

(a)  under a rule of Part 2, except rule 14, by clearly displaying flag Y immediately after an incident in which she was involved;

(b)  under any rule not listed in rule C6.1(a) or C6.2 by clearly displaying a red flag as soon as possible after the incident.

**C6.2**  A boat may not protest another boat under

(a)  rule 14, unless damage or injury results;

(b)  a rule of Part 2, unless she was involved in the incident;

(c)  rule 31 or 42; or

(d)  rule C4 or C7.

**C6.3**  A boat intending to request redress because of circumstances that arise before she *finishes* or retires shall clearly display a red flag as soon as possible after she becomes aware of those circumstances, but no later than two minutes after *finishing* or retiring.

**C6.4**  (a)  A boat protesting under rule C6.1(a) shall remove flag Y before or as soon as possible after the umpires' signal.

(b)  A boat protesting under rule C6.1(b) or requesting redress under rule C6.3 shall, for her *protest* or request to be valid, keep her red flag displayed until she has so informed the umpires after *finishing* or retiring. No written *protest* or request for redress is required.

**C6.5** **Umpire Decisions**

(a) After flag Y is displayed, the umpires shall decide whether to penalize any boat. They shall signal their decision in compliance with rule C5.1, C5.2 or C5.3. However, when the umpires penalize a boat under rule C8.2 and in the same incident there is a flag Y from a boat, the umpires may disregard the flag Y.

(b) The red-flag penalty in rule C5.3 shall be used when a boat has gained a controlling position as a result of breaking a *rule*, but the umpires are not certain that the conditions for an additional umpire-initiated penalty have been fulfilled.

**C6.6** **Protest Committee Decisions**

(a) The protest committee may take evidence in any way it considers appropriate and may communicate its decision orally.

(b) If the protest committee decides that a breach of a *rule* has had no significant effect on the outcome of the match, it may

(1) impose a penalty of one point or part of one point;

(2) order a resail; or

(3) make another arrangement it decides is equitable, which may be to impose no penalty.

(c) The penalty for breaking rule 14 when damage or injury results will be at the discretion of the protest committee, and may include exclusion from further races in the event.

**C6.7** Add new rule N1.10 to Appendix N:

**N1.10** In rule N.1, one International Umpire may be appointed to the jury, or a panel of it, in place of one International Judge.

**C7** **PENALTY SYSTEM**

**C7.1** **Deleted Rule**

Rule 44 is deleted.

**C7.2**    **All Penalties**

(a)    A penalized boat may delay taking a penalty within the limitations of rule C7.3 and shall take it as follows:

    (1)    When on a leg of the course to a windward *mark*, she shall gybe and, as soon as reasonably possible, luff to a close-hauled course.

    (2)    When on a leg of the course to a leeward *mark* or the finishing line, she shall tack and, as soon as reasonably possible, bear away to a course that is more than ninety degrees from the true wind.

(b)    Add to rule 2: 'When *racing*, a boat need not take a penalty unless signalled to do so by an umpire.'

(c)    A boat completes a leg of the course when her bow crosses the extension of the line from the previous *mark* through the *mark* she is rounding, or on the last leg when she *finishes*.

(d)    A penalized boat shall not be recorded as having *finished* until she takes her penalty and sails completely to the course side of the line and then *finishes*, unless the penalty is cancelled before or after she crosses the finishing line.

(e)    If a boat has one or two outstanding penalties and the other boat in her match is penalized, one penalty for each boat shall be cancelled except that a red-flag penalty shall not cancel or be cancelled by another penalty.

(f)    If a boat has more than two outstanding penalties, the umpires shall signal her disqualification under rule C5.4.

**C7.3**    **Penalty Limitations**

(a)    A boat taking a penalty that includes a tack shall have the spinnaker head below the main-boom gooseneck from the time she passes head to wind until she is on a close-hauled course.

(b)    No part of a penalty may be taken inside the *zone* of a rounding *mark* that begins, bounds or ends the leg the boat is on.

(c)    If a boat has one outstanding penalty, she may take the penalty any time after *starting* and before *finishing*. If a boat has two outstanding penalties, she shall take one of them as soon as reasonably possible, but not before *starting*.

(d)   When the umpires display a red flag with or soon after a penalty flag, the penalized boat shall take a penalty as soon as reasonably possible, but not before *starting*.

**C7.4    Taking and Completing Penalties**

(a)   When a boat with an outstanding penalty is on a leg to a windward *mark* and gybes, or is on a leg to a leeward *mark* or the finishing line and passes head to wind, she is taking a penalty.

(b)   When a boat taking a penalty either does not take the penalty correctly or does not complete the penalty as soon as reasonably possible, she is no longer taking a penalty. The umpires shall signal this as required by rule C5.6.

(c)   The umpire boat for each match shall display blue or yellow flags or shapes, each flag or shape indicating one outstanding penalty. When a boat has taken a penalty, or a penalty has been cancelled, one flag or shape shall be removed, with the appropriate sound signal. Failure of the umpires to signal correctly shall not change the number of penalties outstanding.

**C8      PENALTIES INITIATED BY UMPIRES**

**C8.1    Rule Changes**

(a)   Rules 60.2(a) and 60.3(a) do not apply to *rules* for which penalties may be imposed by umpires.

(b)   Rule 64.1(a) is changed so that the provision for exonerating a boat may be applied by the umpires without a hearing, and it takes precedence over any conflicting rule of this appendix.

**C8.2**   When the umpires decide that a boat has broken rule 31, 42, C4, C7.3(c) or C7.3(d) she shall be penalized by signalling her under rule C5.2 or C5.3. However, if a boat is penalized for breaking a rule of Part 2 and if she in the same incident breaks rule 31, she shall not be penalized for breaking rule 31. Furthermore, a boat that displays an incorrect flag or does not display the correct flag shall be warned orally and given an opportunity to correct the error before being penalized.

**C8.3**    When the umpires decide that a boat has

    (a)    gained an advantage by breaking a *rule* after allowing for a penalty,

    (b)    deliberately broken a *rule*, or

    (c)    committed a breach of sportsmanship,

    she shall be penalized under rule C5.2, C5.3 or C5.4.

**C8.4**    If the umpires or protest committee members decide that a boat may have broken a *rule* other than those listed in rules C6.1(a) and C6.2, they shall so inform the protest committee for its action under rule 60.3 and rule C6.6 when appropriate.

**C8.5**    When, after one boat has *started*, the umpires are satisfied that the other boat will not *start*, they may signal under rule C5.4 that the boat that did not *start* is disqualified and the match is terminated.

**C8.6**    When the match umpires, together with at least one other umpire, decide that a boat has broken rule 14 and damage resulted, they may impose a points-penalty without a hearing. The competitor shall be informed of the penalty as soon as practicable and, at the time of being so informed, may request a hearing. The protest committee shall then proceed under rule C6.6. Any penalty decided by the protest committee may be more than the penalty imposed by the umpires. When the umpires decide that a penalty greater than one point is appropriate, they shall act under rule C8.4.

**C9**    **REQUESTS FOR REDRESS OR REOPENING; APPEALS; OTHER PROCEEDINGS**

**C9.1**    There shall be no request for redress or an appeal from a decision made under rule C5, C6, C7 or C8. In rule 66 the third sentence is changed to: 'A *party* to the hearing may not ask for a reopening.'

**C9.2**    A competitor may not base a request for redress on a claim that an action by an official boat was improper. The protest committee may decide to consider giving redress in such circumstances but only if it believes that an official boat, including an umpire boat, may have seriously interfered with a competing boat.

**C9.3**    No proceedings of any kind may be taken in relation to any action or non-action by the umpires, except as permitted in rule C9.2.

**C10**    **SCORING**

**C10.1**    The winning competitor of each match scores one point (half a point each for a dead heat); the loser scores no points.

**C10.2**    When a competitor withdraws from part of an event the scores of all completed races shall stand.

**C10.3**    When a single round robin is terminated before completion, or a multiple round robin is terminated during the first round robin, a competitor's score shall be the average points scored per match sailed by the competitor. However, if any of the competitors have completed less than one third of the scheduled matches, the entire round robin shall be disregarded and, if necessary, the event declared void. For the purposes of tie-breaking in rule C11.1(a), a competitor's score shall be the average points scored per match between the tied competitors.

**C10.4**    When a multiple round robin is terminated with an incomplete round robin, only one point shall be available for all the matches sailed between any two competitors, as follows:

| Number of matches completed between any two competitors | Points for each win |
|---|---|
| 1 | One point |
| 2 | Half a point |
| 3 | A third of a point |
| (etc.) | |

**C10.5**    In a round-robin series,

(a)    competitors shall be placed in order of their total scores, highest score first;

(b)    a competitor who has won a match but is disqualified for breaking a *rule* against a competitor in another match shall lose the point for that match (but the losing competitor shall not be awarded the point); and

(c)    the overall position between competitors who have sailed in different groups shall be decided by the highest score.

**C10.6**    In a knockout series the sailing instructions shall state the minimum number of points required to win a series between two competitors.

When a knockout series is terminated it shall be decided in favour of the competitor with the higher score.

**C11    TIES**

**C11.1    Round-Robin Series**

*In a round-robin series competitors are assigned to one or more groups and scheduled to sail against all other competitors in their group one or more times. Each separate stage identified in the event format shall be a separate round-robin series irrespective of the number of times each competitor sails against each other competitor in that stage.*

Ties between two or more competitors in a round-robin series shall be broken by the following methods, in order, until all ties are broken. When one or more ties are only partially broken, rules C11.1(a) to C11.1(e) shall be reapplied to them. Ties shall be decided in favour of the competitor(s) who

(a)    placed in order, has the highest score in the matches between the tied competitors;

(b)    when the tie is between two competitors in a multiple round robin, has won the last match between the two competitors;

(c)    has the most points against the competitor placed highest in the round-robin series or, if necessary, second highest, and so on until the tie is broken. When two separate ties have to be resolved but the resolution of each depends upon resolving the other, the following principles shall be used in the rule C11.1(c) procedure:

(1)    the higher-place tie shall be resolved before the lower-place tie, and

(2)    all the competitors in the lower-place tie shall be treated as a single competitor for the purposes of rule C11.1(c);

(d)    after applying rule C10.5(c), has the highest place in the different groups, irrespective of the number of competitors in each group;

(e)    has the highest place in the most recent stage of the event (fleet race, round robin, etc.).

**C11.2    Knockout Series**

Ties (including 0–0) between competitors in a knockout series shall be broken by the following methods, in order, until the tie is broken. The tie shall be decided in favour of the competitor who

(a)    has the highest place in the most recent round-robin series, applying rule C11.1 if necessary;

(b)    has won the most recent match in the event between the tied competitors.

**C11.3    Remaining Ties**

When rule C11.1 or C11.2 does not resolve a tie,

(a)    if the tie needs to be resolved for a later stage of the event (or another event for which the event is a direct qualifier), the tie shall be broken by a sail-off when practicable. When the race committee decides that a sail-off is not practicable, the tie shall be decided in favour of the competitor who has the highest score in the round-robin series after eliminating the score for the first race for each tied competitor or, should this fail to break the tie, the second race for each tied competitor and so on until the tie is broken. When a tie is partially resolved, the remaining tie shall be broken by reapplying rule C11.1 or C11.2.

(b)    to decide the winner of an event that is not a direct qualifier for another event, or the overall position between competitors eliminated in one round of a knockout series, a sail-off may be used (but not a draw).

(c)    when a tie is not broken any monetary prizes or ranking points for tied places shall be added together and divided equally among the tied competitors.

# APPENDIX D
# TEAM RACING RULES

*Team races shall be sailed under* The Racing Rules of Sailing *as changed by this appendix.*

**D1** **CHANGES TO THE RACING RULES**

**D1.1** **Definitions and the Rules of Parts 2 and 4**

(a) In the definition *Zone* the distance is changed to two hull lengths.

(b) Rule 18.2(b) is changed to:

If boats are *overlapped* when the first of them reaches the *zone*, the outside boat at that moment shall thereafter give the inside boat *mark-room*. If a boat is *clear ahead* when she reaches the *zone*, or she later becomes *clear ahead* when another boat passes head to wind, the boat *clear astern* at that moment shall thereafter give her *mark-room*.

(c) Rule 18.4 is deleted.

(d) When rule 20 applies the following arm signals by the helmsman are required in addition to the hails:

(1) for 'Room to tack', repeatedly and clearly pointing to windward; and

(2) for 'You tack', repeatedly and clearly pointing at the other boat and waving the arm to windward.

Sailing instructions may delete this requirement.

(e) Rule 24.1 is changed to: 'If reasonably possible, a boat not *racing* shall not interfere with a boat that is *racing*, and a boat that has *finished* shall not act to interfere with a boat that has not *finished*.'

(f) Add new rule 24.3: 'When boats in different races meet, any change of course by either boat shall be consistent with complying with a *rule* or trying to win her own race.'

(g) Add to rule 41:

(e) help from another boat on her team provided electronic communication is not used

(h) Rule 45 is deleted.

**D1.2    Protests and Requests for Redress**

(a)    Rule 60.1 is changed to:

A boat may

(a)    protest another boat, but not for an alleged breach of a rule of Part 2 unless she was involved in the incident or the incident involved contact between members of the other team; or

(b)    request redress.

(b)    Rule 61.1(a) is changed so that a boat may remove her red flag after it has been conspicuously displayed.

(c)    A boat intending to request redress for an incident in the racing area shall display a red flag at the first reasonable opportunity after the incident. She shall display the red flag until it is acknowledged by the race committee or by an umpire.

(d)    The race committee or protest committee shall not protest a boat for breaking a rule of Part 2 or rule 31 or 42 except

(1)    based on evidence in a report from an umpire after a black and white flag has been displayed; or

(2)    under rule 14 upon receipt of a report from any source alleging damage or injury.

(e)    *Protests* and requests for redress need not be in writing. The protest committee may take evidence in any way it considers appropriate and may communicate its decision orally.

(f)    A boat is not entitled to redress based on damage or injury caused by another boat on her team.

(g)    When a supplied boat suffers a breakdown, rule D5 applies.

**D1.3    Penalties**

(a)    Rule 44.1 is changed to:

A boat may take a One-Turn Penalty when she may have broken one or more rules of Part 2, or rule 31 or 42, in an incident while *racing*. However, when she may have broken a rule of Part 2 and rule 31 in the same incident she need not take the penalty for breaking rule 31.

(b)    A boat may take a penalty by retiring, in which case she shall notify the race committee as soon as possible and 6 points shall be added to her score.

(c)    There shall be no penalty for breaking a rule of Part 2 when the incident is between boats on the same team and there is no contact.

## D2    UMPIRED RACES

### D2.1    When Rule D2 Applies

Rule D2 applies to umpired races. Races to be umpired shall be identified either in the sailing instructions or by the display of flag J no later than the warning signal.

### D2.2    Protests by Boats

When a boat protests under a rule of Part 2 or under rule 31 or 42 for an incident in the racing area, she is not entitled to a hearing and the following applies:

(a)    She shall hail 'Protest' and conspicuously display a red flag at the first reasonable opportunity for each.

(b)    The boats shall be given time to respond. A boat involved in the incident may respond by promptly taking an appropriate penalty or clearly indicating that she will do so as soon as possible.

(c)    If no boat takes a penalty, an umpire shall decide whether to penalize any boat.

(d)    If more than one boat broke a rule and was not exonerated, an umpire may penalize any boat that broke a rule and did not take an appropriate penalty.

(e)    An umpire shall signal a decision in compliance with rule D2.4.

(f)    A boat penalized by an umpire shall take a Two-Turns Penalty.

### D2.3    Penalties Initiated by an Umpire

An umpire may penalize a boat without a *protest* by another boat, or report the incident to the protest committee, or both, when the boat

(a)    breaks rule 31 or 42 and does not take a penalty;

(b)    breaks a rule of Part 2 and makes contact with another boat on her team or with a boat in another race, and no boat takes a penalty;

(c) breaks a *rule* and her team gains an advantage despite her, or another boat on her team, taking a penalty;

(d) breaks rule 14 and there is damage or injury;

(e) clearly indicates that she will take a One-Turn Penalty, and then fails to do so;

(f) fails to take a penalty signalled by an umpire;

(g) commits a breach of sportsmanship.

The umpire shall signal a decision in compliance with rule D2.4. A boat penalized by an umpire shall take a Two-Turns Penalty except that, when an umpire hails a number of turns, the boat shall take that number of One-Turn Penalties.

**D2.4    Signals by an Umpire**

An umpire shall signal a decision with one long sound and the display of a flag as follows:

(a) For no penalty, a green and white flag.

(b) To penalize one or more boats, a red flag. The umpire shall hail or signal to identify each boat penalized.

(c) To report the incident to the protest committee, a black and white flag.

**D2.5    Two-Flag Protest Procedure**

*This rule applies only if the sailing instructions so state and it then replaces rule D2.2.*

When a boat protests under a rule of Part 2 or under rule 31 or 42 for an incident in the racing area, she is not entitled to a hearing and the following applies:

(a) She shall hail 'Protest' and conspicuously display a red flag at the first reasonable opportunity for each.

(b) The boats shall be given time to respond. A boat involved in the incident may respond by promptly taking an appropriate penalty or clearly indicating that she will do so as soon as possible.

(c) If the protested boat fails to respond, the protesting boat may request a decision by conspicuously displaying a yellow flag and hailing 'Umpire'.

(d)   An umpire shall then decide whether to penalize any boat.

(e)   An umpire shall signal a decision in compliance with rule D2.4.

(f)   If a boat hails for an umpire decision without complying with the protest procedure, an umpire shall signal No Penalty.

(g)   A boat penalized by an umpire shall take a Two-Turns Penalty.

## D2.6     Limited Umpiring

*This rule applies only if the sailing instructions so state and it then changes rules D2.2 and D2.5.*

When a boat protests and either there is no decision signalled, or an umpire displays a yellow flag with one long sound signalling he has insufficient facts to make a decision, the protesting boat is entitled to a hearing.

## D2.7     Limitations on Other Proceedings

A decision, action or non-action of an umpire shall not be

(a)   grounds for redress,

(b)   subject to an appeal under rule 70, or

(c)   grounds for *abandoning* a race after it has started.

The protest committee may decide to consider giving redress when it believes that an official boat, including an umpire boat, may have seriously interfered with a competing boat.

## D3     SCORING A RACE

### D3.1

(a)   Each boat *finishing* a race shall be scored points equal to her finishing place. All other boats shall be scored points equal to the number of boats entitled to *race*.

(b)   When a boat is scored OCS, 10 points shall be added to her score unless she retired as soon as possible after the starting signal.

(c)   When a boat fails to take a penalty imposed by an umpire at or near the finishing line, she shall be scored points for last place and other scores shall be adjusted accordingly.

(d)   When a protest committee decides that a boat that is a *party* to a protest hearing has broken a *rule* and is not exonerated,

    (1)   if the boat has not taken a penalty, 6 points shall be added to her score;

    (2)   if the boat's team has gained an advantage despite any penalty taken or imposed, the boat's score may be increased;

    (3)   when the boat has broken rule 1 or 2, rule 14 when she has caused damage or injury, or a *rule* when not *racing*, half or more race wins may be deducted from her team, or no penalty may be imposed. Race wins deducted shall not be awarded to any other team.

**D3.2**   When all boats on one team have *finished*, retired or failed to *start*, the other team's boats *racing* at that time shall be scored the points they would have received had they *finished*.

**D3.3**   The team with the lower total points wins the race. If the totals are equal, the team that does not have first place wins.

**D4**   **SCORING A STAGE**

**D4.1**   **Terminology**

(a)   The racing format at an event will consist of one or more stages.

(b)   In a round-robin stage teams are assigned to one or more groups and scheduled to sail one or more round-robins. A round robin is a schedule of races in which each team sails once against each other team in the same group.

(c)   In a knock-out stage teams are scheduled to sail in matches. A match is one or more races between two teams.

(d)   The notice of race or sailing instructions may specify other formats and scoring methods.

**D4.2**   **Terminating a Stage**

(a)   The race committee may terminate a stage at any reasonable time taking into account the entries, weather, time constraints and other relevant factors.

(b)  When a round-robin stage is terminated, any round-robin in the stage in which 80% or more of the full schedule of races has been completed shall be scored as complete; if fewer races have been completed, the round-robin shall not be scored, but may be used to break ties.

**D4.3    Scoring a Round-Robin Stage**

(a)  In a round-robin stage the teams shall be ranked in order of number of race wins, highest number first. If the teams have not completed an equal number of races, they shall be ranked in order of the percentage of races won, highest number first.

(b)  If a round-robin in the stage is not completed, teams shall be ranked according to the results from all completed round-robins in the stage.

**D4.4    Ties in a Completed Round-Robin Stage**

Ties in a completed round-robin stage shall be broken by using, in the following order, only results in the stage,

(a)  the highest number of race wins in all races between the tied teams;

(b)  the lowest total points scored in all races between the tied teams;

(c)  if two teams remain tied, the winner of the last race between them;

(d)  the lowest average points scored in all races against common opponents;

(e)  a sail-off if possible, otherwise a game of chance.

If a tie is partially broken by one of these, the remaining tie shall be broken by starting again at rule D4.4(a).

**D4.5    Ties in an Incomplete Round-Robin Stage**

Ties in an incomplete round-robin stage shall be broken whenever possible using the results from races between the tied teams in any incomplete round-robin. Other ties shall be broken in accordance with rule D4.4.

**D4.6    Scoring a Knock-Out Stage**

The winner of a match is the first team to score the number of race wins stated in the sailing instructions.

**D4.7** **Incomplete Knock-Out Stage**

If a match in a knock-out stage is not completed (including 0-0), the result of the match shall be determined using, in order,

(a)  the higher number of race wins in the incomplete match;

(b)  the higher number of race wins in all races in the event between the tied teams;

(c)  the higher place in the most recent stage, applying rule D4.4(a) if necessary;

(d)  the winner of the most recent race between the teams.

If this rule fails to determine a result, the stage shall be tied unless the sailing instructions provide for some other result.

**D5** **BREAKDOWNS WHEN BOATS ARE SUPPLIED BY THE ORGANIZING AUTHORITY**

**D5.1** Rule D5 applies when boats are supplied by the organizing authority.

**D5.2** When a boat suffers a breakdown in the racing area, she may request a score change by displaying a red flag at the first reasonable opportunity after the breakdown until it is acknowledged by the race committee or by an umpire. If possible, she shall continue *racing*.

**D5.3** The race committee shall decide requests for a score change in accordance with rules D5.4 and D5.5. It may take evidence in any way it considers appropriate and may communicate its decision orally.

**D5.4** When the race committee decides that the team's finishing position was made significantly worse, that the breakdown was through no fault of the crew, and that in the same circumstances a reasonably competent crew would not have been able to avoid the breakdown, it shall make as equitable a decision as possible. This may be to *abandon* and resail the race or, when the boat's finishing position was predictable, award her points for that position. Any doubt about a boat's position when she broke down shall be resolved against her.

**D5.5** A breakdown caused by defective supplied equipment or a breach of a *rule* by an opponent shall not normally be determined to be the fault of the crew, but one caused by careless handling, capsizing or a breach by a boat on the same team shall be. If there is doubt, it shall be presumed that the crew are not at fault.

# APPENDIX E
## RADIO SAILING RACING RULES

*Radio sailing races shall be sailed under* The Racing Rules of Sailing *as changed by this appendix.*

**E1    CHANGES TO THE DEFINITIONS, TERMINOLOGY AND THE RULES OF PARTS 1, 2 AND 7**

**E1.1    Definitions**

Add to the definition *Conflict of Interest*:

> However, an observer does not have a *conflict of interest* solely by being a competitor.

In the definition *Zone* the distance is changed to four hull lengths.

Add new definition:

> **Disabled**    A boat is *disabled* while she is unable to continue in the heat.

**E1.2    Terminology**

The Terminology paragraph of the Introduction is changed so that:

(a)    'Boat' means a sailboat controlled by radio signals and having no crew. However, in the rules of Part 1 and Part 5, rule E6 and the definitions *Party* and *Protest*, 'boat' includes the competitor controlling her.

(b)    'Competitor' means the person designated to control a boat using radio signals.

(c)    In the racing rules, but not in its appendices, replace the noun 'race' with 'heat'. In Appendix E a race consists of one or more heats and is completed when the last heat in the race is completed.

**E1.3    Rules of Parts 1, 2 and 7**

(a)    Rule 1.2 is deleted.

(b)    In rule 20, hails and replies shall be made by the competitor controlling the boat.

(c) Rule 23 is changed to: 'If possible, a boat shall avoid a boat that is *disabled*.'

(d) Rule 90.2(c) is changed to:

Changes to the sailing instructions may be communicated orally to all affected competitors before the warning signal of the relevant race or heat. When appropriate, changes shall be confirmed in writing.

## E2     ADDITIONAL RULES WHEN RACING

*Rule E2 applies only while boats are **racing**.*

### E2.1     Hailing Requirements

(a) A hail shall be made so that the competitors to whom the hail is directed might reasonably be expected to hear it.

(b) The individual digits of a boat's sail number shall be hailed; for example 'one five', not 'fifteen'.

### E2.2     Giving Advice

A competitor shall not give tactical or strategic advice to a competitor controlling a boat that is *racing*.

### E2.3     Boat Out of Radio Control

A competitor who loses radio control of his boat shall promptly hail and repeat '(The boat's sail number) out of control' and the boat shall retire.

### E2.4     Transmitter Aerials

If a transmitter aerial is longer than 200mm when extended, the extremity shall be adequately protected.

### E2.5     Radio Interference

Transmission of radio signals that cause interference with the control of other boats is prohibited. A competitor that has broken this rule shall not *race* again until permitted to do so by the race committee.

## E3     CONDUCT OF A RACE

### E3.1     Control Area

The sailing instructions may specify a control area; if not specified, it shall be unrestricted. Competitors shall be in this area when controlling boats that are *racing*, except briefly to handle and then release or relaunch the boat.

**E3.2    Launching Area**

The sailing instructions may specify a launching area and its use; if not specified it shall be unrestricted.

**E3.3    Course Board**

The sailing instructions may require the course to be displayed on a board and, if so, the board shall be located in or adjacent to the control area.

**E3.4    Starting and Finishing**

(a)   Rule 26 is changed to:

Heats shall be started using warning, preparatory and starting signals at one-minute intervals. During the minute before the starting signal, additional sound or oral signals shall be made at ten-second intervals, and during the final ten seconds at one-second intervals. Each signal shall be timed from the beginning of its sound.

(b)   The starting and finishing lines shall be between the course sides of the starting and finishing *marks*.

**E3.5    Individual Recall**

Rule 29.1 is changed to:

When at a boat's starting signal any part of the boat is on the course side of the starting line or when she must comply with rule 30.1, the race committee shall promptly hail 'Recall (sail numbers)' and repeat the hail as appropriate. If rule 30.3 or 30.4 applies this rule does not.

**E3.6    General Recall**

Rule 29.2 is changed to:

When at the starting signal the race committee is unable to identify boats that are on the course side of the starting line or to which rule 30 applies, or there has been an error in the starting procedure, the race committee may hail and repeat as appropriate 'General recall' and make two loud sounds. The warning signal for a new start will normally be made shortly thereafter.

**E3.7      U Flag and Black Flag Rules**

When the race committee informs a boat that she has broken rule 30.3 or 30.4, the boat shall immediately leave the course area.

**E3.8      Other Changes to the Rules of Part 3**

(a)   Rules 30.2 and 33 are deleted.

(b)   All race committee signals shall be made orally or by other sounds. No visual signals are required unless specified in the sailing instructions.

(c)   Courses shall not be shortened.

(d)   Rule 32.1(a) is changed to: 'because of foul weather or thunderstorms,'.

**E3.9      Disabled Competitors**

To enable a disabled competitor to compete on equal terms, the race committee shall make as fair an arrangement as possible.

**E4      RULES OF PART 4**

**E4.1      Deleted Rules in Part 4**

Rules 40, 43, 44.3, 45, 47, 48, 49, 50, 52 and 54 are deleted.

**E4.2      Outside Help**

Rule 41 is changed to:

A boat or the competitor controlling her shall not receive help from any outside source, except

(a)   help needed as a direct result of a competitor becoming ill, injured or in danger;

(b)   when the boat is entangled with another boat, help from the other competitor;

(c)   when the boat is entangled, or she is aground or in danger, help from a race committee vessel;

(d)   help in the form of information freely available to all competitors;

(e)   unsolicited information from a disinterested source. A competitor is not a disinterested source unless acting as an observer.

However, a boat that gains a significant advantage in the heat or race from help received under rule 41 may be protested and penalized; any penalty may be less than disqualification.

### E4.3    Taking a Penalty

Rule 44.1 is changed to:

A boat may take a One-Turn Penalty when she may have broken one or more rules of Part 2, or rule 31, in an incident while *racing*. However,

(a)    when she may have broken a rule of Part 2 and rule 31 in the same incident she need not take the penalty for breaking rule 31;

(b)    if the boat gained a significant advantage in the heat or race by her breach despite taking a penalty, her penalty shall be an additional One-Turn Penalty;

(c)    if the boat caused serious damage, or as a result of breaking a rule of Part 2 she caused another boat to become *disabled* and retire, her penalty shall be to retire.

### E4.4    Person in Charge

Rule 46 is changed to: 'The member or organization that entered the boat shall designate the competitor. See rule 75.'

## E5    RACING WITH OBSERVERS AND UMPIRES

### E5.1    Observers

(a)    The race committee may appoint observers, who may be competitors.

(b)    Observers shall hail the sail numbers of boats that make contact with a *mark* or another boat and shall repeat the hail as appropriate.

(c)    At the end of a heat, observers shall report to the race committee all unresolved incidents, and any failure to sail the course as required by rule 28.

**E5.2     Umpired Races**

The International Radio Sailing Association Addendum Q shall apply to umpired races. Races to be umpired may be identified in the sailing instructions or orally before the warning signal.

*Note: The addendum is available at the website: **radiosailing.org**.*

**E5.3     Rules for Observers and Umpires**

Observers and umpires shall be located in the control area. They shall not use any aid or device that gives them a visual advantage over competitors.

**E6      PROTESTS AND REQUESTS FOR REDRESS**

**E6.1     Right to Protest**

Rule 60.1 is changed to:

A boat may

(a)   protest another boat, but not for an alleged breach of a rule of Part 2, 3 or 4 unless she was scheduled to sail in that heat; or

(b)   request redress.

However, a boat or competitor may not protest for an alleged breach of rules E2 or E3.7.

**E6.2     Protest for a Rule Broken by a Competitor**

When a race committee or protest committee learns that a competitor may have broken a *rule*, it may protest the boat controlled by that competitor.

**E6.3     Informing the Protestee**

Rule 61.1(a) is changed to:

A boat intending to protest shall inform the other boat at the first reasonable opportunity. When her *protest* concerns an incident in the racing area that she was involved in or saw, she shall hail twice '(Her own sail number) protest (the sail number of the other boat)'.

**E6.4     Informing the Race Committee**

A boat intending to protest or request redress about an incident in the racing area or control area shall inform the race officer as soon as reasonably possible after *finishing* or retiring.

**E6.5    Time Limits**

A *protest*, request for redress or request for reopening shall be delivered to the race officer no later than ten minutes after the last boat in the heat *finishes* or after the relevant incident, whichever is later.

**E6.6    Redress**

Add to rule 62.1:

(e)    external radio interference acknowledged by the race committee, or

(f)    becoming *disabled* because of the action of a boat that was breaking a rule of Part 2 or of a vessel not *racing* that was required to keep clear.

**E6.7    Right to Be Present**

In rule 63.3(a) 'the representatives of boats shall have been on board' is changed to 'the representative of each boat shall be the competitor designated to control her'.

**E6.8    Taking Evidence and Finding Facts**

Add to rule 63.6:

When the *protest* concerns an alleged breach of a rule of Part 2, 3 or 4, any witness shall have been in the control area at the time of the incident. If the witness is a competitor who was not acting as an observer, he shall also have been scheduled to race in the relevant heat.

**E6.9    Decisions on Redress**

Add to rule 64.2:

If a boat is given redress because she was damaged, her redress shall include reasonable time, but not more than 30 minutes, to make repairs before her next heat.

**E7     PENALTIES**

When a protest committee decides that a boat that is a *party* to a protest hearing has broken a *rule* other than a rule of Part 2, 3 or 4, it shall either

(a)   disqualify her or add any number of points (including zero and fractions of points) to her score. The penalty shall be applied, if possible, to the heat or race in which the *rule* was broken; otherwise it shall be applied to the next heat or race for that boat. When points are added, the scores of other boats shall not be changed; or

(b)   require her to take one or more One-Turn Penalties that shall be taken as soon as possible after the starting signal of her next heat that is started and not subsequently recalled or *abandoned*.

However, if the boat has broken a rule in Appendix G or rule E8, the protest committee shall act in accordance with rule G4.

**E8     CHANGES TO APPENDIX G, IDENTIFICATION ON SAILS**

Rule G1, except the table of National Sail Letters, is changed to:

**G1   WORLD SAILING AND IRSA CLASS BOATS**

*This rule applies to every boat of a class administered or recognised by World Sailing or by the International Radio Sailing Association (IRSA).*

**G1.1  Identification**

(a)   A boat of a World Sailing or IRSA Class shall display her class insignia, national letters and sail number as specified in rule G1, unless her class rules state otherwise.

(b)   At world and continental championships, sails shall comply with these rules. At other events they shall comply with these rules or the rules applicable at the time of their initial certification.

**G1.2  National Letters**

At all international events, a boat shall display national letters in accordance with the table of National Sail Letters denoting:

(a)   when entered under rule 75.1(a), the national authority of the nationality, place of residence, or affiliation of the owner or the member.

(b)   when entered under rule 75.1(b), the national authority of the organisation which entered her.

For the purposes of this rule, international events are world and continental championships and events described as international events in their notices of race and sailing instructions.

*Note: An up-to-date version of the National Sail Letters table is available on the World Sailing website.*

### G1.3  Sail numbers

(a)    The sail number shall be the last two digits of the boat's registration number or the competitor's or owner's personal number, allotted by the relevant issuing authority.

(b)    When there is conflict between sail numbers, or when a sail number may be misread, the race committee shall require that the sail numbers of one or more boats be changed to numeric alternatives.

### G1.4  Specifications

(a)    National letters and sail numbers shall be in capital letters and Arabic numerals, clearly legible and of the same colour. Commercially available typefaces giving the same or better legibility than Helvetica are acceptable.

(b)    The height and spacing of letters and numbers shall be as follows:

| Dimension | Minimum | Maximum |
|---|---|---|
| Height of sail numbers | 100 mm | 110 mm |
| Spacing of adjacent sail numbers | 20 mm | 30 mm |
| Height of national letters | 60 mm | 70 mm |
| Spacing of adjacent national letters | 13 mm | 23 mm |

### G1.5  Positioning

(a)    Class insignia, sail numbers and national letters shall be positioned

(1)    on both sides of the sail;

(2)    with those on the starboard side uppermost;

(3)    approximately horizontally;

(4)    with no less than 40 mm vertical spacing between numbers and letters on opposite sides of the sail;

(5)     with no less than 20 mm vertical spacing between class insignia on opposite sides of the sail.

However, symmetrical or reversed class insignia may be positioned back to back.

(b)  On a mainsail, sail numbers shall be positioned

(1)     below class insignia;

(2)     above the line perpendicular to the luff through the quarter leech point;

(3)     above national letters;

(4)     with sufficient space in front of the sail number for a prefix '1'.

### G1.6  Exceptions

(a)  Where the size of the sail prevents compliance with rule G1.2, National Letters, then exceptions to rules G1.2, G1.4, and G1.5 shall be made in the following order of precedence. National letters shall

(1)     be spaced vertically below sail numbers by less than 30 mm, but no less than 20 mm;

(2)     be spaced on opposite sides of the sail by less than 30 mm, but no less than 20 mm;

(3)     be reduced in height to less than 45 mm, but no less than 40 mm;

(4)     be omitted.

(b)  Where the size of the sail prevents compliance with rule G1.3, Sail Numbers, then exceptions to rules G1.4 and G1.5 shall be made in the following order of precedence. Sail numbers shall

(1)     extend below the specified line;

(2)     be spaced on opposite sides of the sail by less than 30 mm, but no less than 20 mm apart;

(3)     be reduced in height to less than 90 mm, but no less than 80 mm;

(4)     be omitted on all except the largest sail;

(5)     be reduced in height until they do fit on the largest sail.

# APPENDIX F
## KITEBOARD RACING RULES

*Kiteboard course races shall be sailed under* The Racing Rules of Sailing *as changed by this appendix. The term 'boat' elsewhere in the racing rules means 'kiteboard' or 'boat' as appropriate.*

*Note: Rules for other kiteboard racing formats (such as Short Track, Kitecross, Slalom, Boarder X) or other kiteboard competitions (such as Freestyle, Wave, Big Air, Speed) are not included in this appendix. Links to current versions of these rules can be found on the World Sailing website.*

### CHANGES TO THE DEFINITIONS

The definitions *Clear Astern* and *Clear Ahead*; *Overlap*, *Finish*, *Keep Clear*, *Leeward* and *Windward*, *Mark-Room*, *Obstruction*, *Start*, *Tack*, *Starboard* or *Port* and *Zone* are changed to:

**Clear Astern and Clear Ahead; Overlap**  One kiteboard is *clear astern* of another when her hull is behind a line abeam from the aftermost point of the other kiteboard's hull. The other kiteboard is *clear ahead*. They *overlap* when neither is *clear astern*. However, they also *overlap* when a kiteboard between them *overlaps* both. These terms always apply to kiteboards on the same *tack*. They do not apply to kiteboards on opposite *tacks* unless both kiteboards are sailing more than ninety degrees from the true wind.

**Finish**  A kiteboard *finishes* when, while the competitor is in contact with the hull, any part of her hull, or the competitor in normal position, crosses the finishing line from the course side. However, she has not *finished* if after crossing the finishing line she

(a)    takes a penalty under rule 44.2,

(b)    corrects an error under rule 28.2 made at the line, or

(c)    continues to sail the course.

**Keep Clear**  A kiteboard *keeps clear* of a right-of-way kiteboard

(a)    if the right-of-way kiteboard can sail her course with no need to take avoiding action and,

(b)    when the kiteboards are *overlapped*, if the right-of-way kiteboard can also, without immediately making contact, change course in both directions or move her kite in any direction.

**Leeward and Windward**  A kiteboard's *leeward* side is the side that is or, when she is head to wind, was away from the wind. However, when sailing by the lee or directly downwind, her *leeward* side is the side on which her kite lies. The other side is her *windward* side. When two kiteboards on the same *tack overlap*, the one whose hull is on the *leeward* side of the other's hull is the *leeward* kiteboard. The other is the *windward* kiteboard.

**Mark-Room**  *Room* for a kiteboard to sail her *proper course* to round or pass the *mark* on the required side.

**Obstruction**  An object that a kiteboard could not pass without changing course substantially, if she were sailing directly towards it and 10 metres from it. An object that can be safely passed on only one side and an area so designated by the sailing instructions are also *obstructions*. However, a kiteboard *racing* is not an *obstruction* to other kiteboards unless they are required to *keep clear* of her or, if rule 23 applies, avoid her. A vessel under way, including a kiteboard *racing*, is never a continuing *obstruction*.

**Start**  A kiteboard *starts* when, her hull and the competitor having been entirely on the pre-start side of the starting line at or after her starting signal, and having complied with rule 30.1 if it applies, any part of her hull, or the competitor crosses the starting line in the direction of the first *mark*.

**Tack, Starboard or Port**  A kiteboard is on the *tack*, *starboard* or *port*, corresponding to the competitor's hand that would be forward if the competitor were in normal riding position (riding heel side with both hands on the control bar and arms not crossed). A kiteboard is on *starboard tack* when the competitor's right hand would be forward and is on the *port tack* when the competitor's left hand would be forward.

**Zone**  The area around a *mark* within a distance of 30 metres. A kiteboard is in the *zone* when any part of her hull is in the *zone*.

Add the following definitions:

**Capsized**  A kiteboard is *capsized* if

(a)    her kite is in the water,

(b)    her lines are tangled with another kiteboard's lines, or

(c)    the competitor has, clearly by accident and for a significant period of time,

(1)    fallen into the water or

(2)    become disconnected from the hull.

**Jumping**  A kiteboard is *jumping* when her hull, its appendages and the competitor are clear of the water.

**Recovering**  A kiteboard is *recovering* from the time her kite is out of the water until she has steerage way.

## F1    CHANGES TO THE RULES OF PART 1

*[No changes.]*

## F2    CHANGES TO THE RULES OF PART 2

### PART 2 - PREAMBLE

In the second sentence of the preamble, 'injury or serious damage' is changed to 'injury, serious damage or a tangle'.

### 13    WHILE TACKING

Rule 13 is deleted.

### 14    AVOIDING CONTACT

Rule 14(b) is changed to:

(b)    shall be exonerated if she breaks this rule and the contact does not cause damage, injury or a tangle.

### 16    CHANGING COURSE OR KITE POSITION

Rule 16 is changed to:

**16.1** When a right-of-way kiteboard changes course or the position of her kite, she shall give the other kiteboard *room* to *keep clear*.

**16.2** In addition, when after the starting signal a *port-tack* kiteboard is *keeping clear* by sailing to pass astern of a *starboard-tack* kiteboard, the *starboard-tack* kiteboard shall not change course or the position of her kite if as a result the *port-tack* kiteboard would immediately need to change course or the position of her kite to continue *keeping clear*.

## 17  ON THE SAME TACK; PROPER COURSE

Rule 17 is deleted.

## 18  MARK-ROOM

Rule 18 is changed to:

### 18.1 When Rule 18 Applies

Rule 18 applies between kiteboards when they are required to leave a *mark* on the same side and at least one of them is in the *zone*. However, it does not apply

(a) between a kiteboard approaching a *mark* and one leaving it, or

(b) between kiteboards on opposite *tacks*.

### 18.2 Giving Mark-Room

(a) When the first kiteboard reaches the *zone*,

   (1) if kiteboards are *overlapped*, the outside kiteboard at that moment shall thereafter give the inside kiteboard *mark-room*.

   (2) if kiteboards are not *overlapped*, the kiteboard that has not reached the *zone* shall thereafter give *mark-room*.

(b) If the kiteboard entitled to *mark-room* leaves the *zone*, the entitlement to *mark-room* ceases and rule 18.2(a) is applied again if required based on the relationship of the kiteboards at the time rule 18.2(a) is re-applied.

(c) If a kiteboard obtained an inside *overlap* and, from the time the *overlap* began, the outside kiteboard is unable to give *mark-room*, she is not required to give it.

## 18.3 Tacking and Gybing

When an inside *overlapped* right-of-way kiteboard must change *tack* at a *mark* to sail her *proper course*, until she changes *tack* she shall sail no farther from the *mark* than needed to sail that course. Rule 18.3 does not apply at a gate *mark* or a finishing *mark* and a kiteboard shall not be penalized for breaking this rule unless the course of another kiteboard was affected by the breach of this rule.

## 20    ROOM TO TACK AT AN OBSTRUCTION

Add new rule 20.4:

## 20.4 Arm Signals

The following arm signals are required in addition to the hails

(a)  for 'Room to tack', repeatedly and clearly circling one hand over the head; and

(b)  for 'You tack', repeatedly and clearly pointing at the other kiteboard and waving the arm to windward.

## 22    STARTING ERRORS; TAKING PENALTIES; JUMPING

Rule 22.3 is changed and new rule 22.4 is added:

**22.3** During the last minute before her starting signal, a kiteboard that stops, slows down significantly, or one that is not making significant forward progress shall *keep clear* of all others unless she is accidentally *capsized*.

**22.4** A kiteboard that is *jumping* shall *keep clear* of one that is not.

## 23    CAPSIZED; RECOVERING; AGROUND; RESCUING

Rule 23 is changed to:

**23.1** If possible, a kiteboard shall avoid a kiteboard that is *capsized* or has not regained control after *capsizing*, is aground, or is trying to help a person or vessel in danger.

**23.2** A kiteboard that is *recovering* shall *keep clear* of a kiteboard that is not.

## F3    CHANGES TO THE RULES OF PART 3

### 29    RECALLS

In rule 29.1 'crew or equipment' is changed to 'competitor'.

### 30    STARTING PENALTIES

In rules 30.1, 30.2, 30.3 and 30.4, 'crew or equipment' is changed to 'or competitor'.

In rule 30.4, 'sail number' is changed to 'competitor number'.

### 31    TOUCHING A MARK

Rule 31 is changed to:

While *racing*, a kiteboard shall not touch a windward *mark*.

### 36    RACES RESTARTED OR RESAILED

Rule 36(b) is changed to:

(b)    cause a kiteboard to be penalized except under rule 30.2, 30.4 or 69 or under rule 14 when she has caused injury, serious damage or a tangle.

## F4    CHANGES TO THE RULES OF PART 4

### 41    OUTSIDE HELP

Add new rules 41(e) and 41(f):

(e)    help from another competitor in the same race to assist a relaunch;

(f)    help to change equipment, but only in the launching area.

### 42    PROPULSION

Rule 42 is changed to:

A kiteboard shall be propelled only by the action of the wind on the kite, by the action of the water on the hull and by the unassisted actions of the competitor. However, the competitor shall not make significant progress by paddling, swimming or walking.

### 43     COMPETITOR CLOTHING AND EQUIPMENT

Rule 43.1(a) is changed to:

(a) Competitors shall not wear or carry clothing or equipment for the purpose of increasing their weight. However, a competitor may wear a drinking container that shall have a capacity of at least one litre and weigh no more than 1.5 kilograms when full.

### 44     PENALTIES AT THE TIME OF AN INCIDENT

Rules 44.1 and 44.2 are changed to:

#### 44.1  Taking a Penalty

A kiteboard may take a One-Turn Penalty when she may have broken one or more rules of Part 2 or rule 31 in an incident while *racing*. Alternatively, the notice of race or sailing instructions may specify the use of the Scoring Penalty or some other penalty, in which case the specified penalty shall replace the One-Turn Penalty. However,

(a) when a kiteboard may have broken a rule of Part 2 and rule 31 in the same incident she need not take the penalty for breaking rule 31; and

(b) if the kiteboard caused injury, damage or a tangle or, despite taking a penalty, gained a significant advantage in the race or series by her breach, her penalty shall be to retire.

#### 44.2  One-Turn Penalty

After getting well clear of other kiteboards as soon after the incident as possible, a kiteboard takes a One-Turn Penalty by promptly making one turn with her hull in the water. The turn shall include one completed tack and one completed gybe. Forward motion shall be established between the tack and the gybe (or vice versa) with the competitor on the correct side of the hull in normal sailing position. When a kiteboard takes the penalty at or near the finishing line, she shall sail completely to the course side of the line before *finishing*.

### PART 4 RULES DELETED

Rules 43.2, 45, 47, 48.1, 49, 50, 51, 52 and 54 are deleted.

## F5    CHANGES TO THE RULES OF PART 5

### 61    PROTEST REQUIREMENTS

Rule 61.1(a) is changed to:

(a)    A kiteboard intending to protest shall inform the other kiteboard at the first reasonable opportunity. When her *protest* will concern an incident in the racing area that she was involved in or saw, she shall hail 'Protest' at the first reasonable opportunity. However,

> (1)    if the other kiteboard is beyond hailing distance, the protesting kiteboard need not hail but she shall inform the other kiteboard at the first reasonable opportunity;

> (2)    no red flag need be displayed;

> (3)    if the incident was an error by the other kiteboard in sailing the course, she need not hail but she shall inform the other kiteboard before that kiteboard *finishes* or at the first reasonable opportunity after she *finishes*;

> (4)    if as a result of the incident either competitor is in danger, or there is injury, serious damage or a tangle that is obvious to the kiteboard intending to protest, the requirements of this rule do not apply to her, but she shall attempt to inform the other kiteboard within the time limit of rule 61.3.

### 62    REDRESS

Rule 62.1(b) is changed to:

(b)    injury, physical damage or a tangle because of the action of a kiteboard that was breaking a rule of Part 2 or of a vessel not *racing* that was required to keep clear;

## 63    HEARINGS

For a race of an elimination series that will qualify a kiteboard to compete in a later stage of an event, rules 61.2 and 65.2 are deleted and rule 63.6 is changed to:

**63.6** *Protests* and requests for redress need not be in writing; they shall be made orally to a member of the protest committee as soon as reasonably possible following the race. The protest committee may take evidence in any way it considers appropriate and may communicate its decision orally.

## 64    DECISIONS

Add new rule 64.1(d):

(d)    when a kiteboard has broken a rule of Part 2 and, as a result, caused a tangle for which redress was given, she shall be scored RCT if she retired or DCT if she was disqualified. When she does this a second or subsequent time in the series, her penalty shall be DNE.

Rules 64.3(a) and 64.3(b) are changed to:

(a)    When the protest committee finds that deviations in excess of acceptable manufacturing tolerances were caused by damage or normal wear and do not improve the performance of the kiteboard, it shall not penalize her. However, the kiteboard shall not *race* again until the deviations have been corrected, except when the protest committee decides there is or has been no reasonable opportunity to do so.

(b)    When the protest committee is in doubt about any matter concerning the measurement of a kiteboard, the interpretation of a class rule, or a matter involving damage to a kiteboard, it shall refer its questions, together with the relevant facts, to an authority responsible for interpreting the rule. In making its decision, the committee shall be bound by the reply of the authority.

**70    APPEALS AND REQUESTS TO A NATIONAL AUTHORITY**

Add new rule 70.7:

**70.7** Appeals are not permitted in disciplines and formats with elimination series.

## F6    CHANGES TO THE RULES OF PART 6

*[No changes.]*

## F7    CHANGES TO THE RULES OF PART 7

**90    RACE COMMITTEE; SAILING INSTRUCTIONS; SCORING**

The last sentence of rule 90.2(c) is changed to: 'Oral instructions may be given only if the procedure is stated in the sailing instructions.'

## F8    CHANGES TO APPENDIX A

**A1    NUMBER OF RACES; OVERALL SCORES**

Rule A1 is changed to:

The number of races scheduled and the number required to be completed to constitute a series shall be stated in the notice of race or sailing instructions. If an event includes more than one discipline or format, the notice of race or sailing instructions shall state how the overall scores are to be calculated.

**A4    LOW POINT SYSTEM**

Rule A4.2 is changed to:

**A4.2** A kiteboard that did not *start*, did not *finish*, retired or was disqualified shall be scored points for the finishing place one more than the number of kiteboards entered in the series or, in a race of an elimination series, the number of kiteboards in that heat. A kiteboard that is penalized under rule 30.2 shall be scored points as provided in rule 44.3(c).

**A11  SCORING ABBREVIATIONS**

Add to Rule A11:

DCT    Disqualified after causing a tangle in an incident

RCT    Retired after causing a tangle

**F9     CHANGES TO APPENDIX G**

Appendix G is changed to:

**Appendix G – Identification on Competitors**

**G1**   Every kiteboard shall be identified as follows:

(a)   Each competitor shall be provided with and wear a shirt with a personal competition number of no more than three digits.

(b)   The numbers shall be displayed on the front and back of the shirts and be at least 15 cm high.

(c)   The numbers shall be Arabic numerals, all of the same solid colour, clearly legible and in a commercially available typeface giving the same or better legibility as Helvetica. The colour of the numbers shall contrast with the colour of the shirt.

# APPENDIX G
# IDENTIFICATION ON SAILS

*See rule 77.*

**R⁄A** **G1**    **WORLD SAILING CLASS BOATS**

**G1.1**    **Identification**

Every boat of a World Sailing Class shall carry on her mainsail and, as provided in rules G1.3(d) and G1.3(e) for letters and numbers only, on her spinnaker and headsail

(a)   the insignia denoting her class;

(b)   at all international events, except when the boats are provided to all competitors, national letters denoting her national authority from the table below. For the purposes of this rule, international events are World Sailing events, world and continental championships, and events described as international events in their notices of race and sailing instructions; and

(c)   a sail number of no more than four digits allotted by her national authority or, when so required by the class rules, by the class association. The four-digit limitation does not apply to classes whose World Sailing membership or recognition took effect before 1 April 1997. Alternatively, if permitted in the class rules, an owner may be allotted a personal sail number by the relevant issuing authority, which may be used on all his boats in that class.

Sails measured before 31 March 1999 shall comply with rule G1.1 or with the rules applicable at the time of measurement.

*Note: An up-to-date version of the table below is available on the World Sailing website.*

## NATIONAL SAIL LETTERS

| National authority | Letters |
|---|---|
| Algeria | ALG |
| American Samoa | ASA |
| Andorra | AND |
| Angola | ANG |
| Antigua | ANT |
| Argentina | ARG |
| Armenia | ARM |
| Aruba | ARU |
| Australia | AUS |
| Austria | AUT |
| Azerbaijan | AZE |
| Bahamas | BAH |
| Bahrain | BRN |
| Barbados | BAR |
| Belarus | BLR |
| Belgium | BEL |
| Belize | BIZ |
| Bermuda | BER |
| Brazil | BRA |
| Brunei Darussalam | BRU |
| British Virgin Islands | IVB |
| Bulgaria | BUL |
| Cambodia | CAM |
| Canada | CAN |
| Cayman Islands | CAY |
| Chile | CHI |
| China, PR | CHN |
| Chinese Taipei | TPE |
| Colombia | COL |
| Cook Islands | COK |
| Croatia | CRO |
| Cuba | CUB |
| Cyprus | CYP |
| Czech Republic | CZE |
| Denmark | DEN |
| Djibouti | DJI |

| National authority | Letters |
|---|---|
| Dominican Republic | DOM |
| Ecuador | ECU |
| Egypt | EGY |
| El Salvador | ESA |
| Estonia | EST |
| Fiji | FIJ |
| Finland | FIN |
| France | FRA |
| Georgia | GEO |
| Germany | GER |
| Great Britain | GBR |
| Greece | GRE |
| Grenada | GRN |
| Guam | GUM |
| Guatemala | GUA |
| Hong Kong | HKG |
| Hungary | HUN |
| Iceland | ISL |
| India | IND |
| Indonesia | INA |
| Iraq | IRQ |
| Ireland | IRL |
| Israel | ISR |
| Italy | ITA |
| Jamaica | JAM |
| Japan | JPN |
| Kazakhstan | KAZ |
| Kenya | KEN |
| Korea, DPR | PRK |
| Korea, Republic of | KOR |
| Kosovo | KOS |
| Kuwait | KUW |
| Kyrgyzstan | KGZ |
| Latvia | LAT |
| Lebanon | LIB |
| Libya | LBA |

| National authority | Letters | National authority | Letters |
|---|---|---|---|
| Liechtenstein | LIE | Samoa | SAM |
| Lithuania | LTU | San Marino | SMR |
| Luxembourg | LUX | Saudi Arabia | KSA |
| Macedonia (FYRO) | MKD | Senegal | SEN |
| Madagascar | MAD | Serbia | SRB |
| Malaysia | MAS | Seychelles | SEY |
| Malta | MLT | Singapore | SGP |
| Mauritius | MRI | Slovak Republic | SVK |
| Mexico | MEX | Slovenia | SLO |
| Moldova | MDA | South Africa | RSA |
| Monaco | MON | Spain | ESP |
| Montenegro | MNE | Sri Lanka | SRI |
| Morocco | MAR | St Lucia | LCA |
| Mozambique | MOZ | St Vincent & Grenadines | VIN |
| Myanmar | MYA | Sudan | SUD |
| Namibia | NAM | Sweden | SWE |
| Netherlands | NED | Switzerland | SUI |
| Netherlands Antilles | AHO | Tahiti | TAH |
| New Zealand | NZL | Tanzania | TAN |
| Nicaragua | NCA | Thailand | THA |
| Nigeria | NGR | Timore Leste | TLS |
| Norway | NOR | Trinidad & Tobago | TTO |
| Oman | OMA | Tunisia | TUN |
| Pakistan | PAK | Turkey | TUR |
| Palestine | PLE | Uganda | UGA |
| Panama | PAN | Ukraine | UKR |
| Papua New Guinea | PNG | United Arab Emirates | UAE |
| Paraguay | PAR | United States of America | USA |
| Peru | PER | Uruguay | URU |
| Philippines | PHI | US Virgin Islands | ISV |
| Poland | POL | Vanuatu | VAN |
| Portugal | POR | Venezuela | VEN |
| Puerto Rico | PUR | Vietnam | VIE |
| Qatar | QAT | Zimbabwe | ZIM |
| Romania | ROU | | |
| Russia | RUS | | |

## G1.2    Specifications

(a)    National letters and sail numbers shall be in capital letters and Arabic numerals, clearly legible and of the same colour. Commercially available typefaces giving the same or better legibility than Helvetica are acceptable.

(b)    The height of characters and space between adjoining characters on the same and opposite sides of the sail shall be related to the boat's overall length as follows:

| Overall length | Minimum height | Minimum space between characters and from edge of sail |
|---|---|---|
| Under 3.5 m | 230 mm | 45 mm |
| 3.5 m – 8.5 m | 300 mm | 60 mm |
| 8.5 m – 11 m | 375 mm | 75 mm |
| Over 11 m | 450 mm | 90 mm |

## G1.3    Positioning

Class insignia, national letters and sail numbers shall be positioned as follows:

(a)    Except as provided in rules G1.3(d) and G1.3(e), class insignia, national letters and sail numbers shall, if possible, be wholly above an arc whose centre is the head point and whose radius is 60% of the leech length. They shall be placed at different heights on the two sides of the sail, those on the starboard side being uppermost.

(b)    The class insignia shall be placed above the national letters. If the class insignia is of such a design that two of them coincide when placed back to back on both sides of the sail, they may be so placed.

(c)    National letters shall be placed above the sail number.

(d)    The national letters and sail number shall be displayed on the front side of a spinnaker but may be placed on both sides. They shall be displayed wholly below an arc whose centre is the head point and whose radius is 40% of the foot median and, if possible, wholly above an arc whose radius is 60% of the foot median.

(e)    The national letters and sail number shall be displayed on both sides of a headsail whose clew can extend behind the mast 30% or more of the mainsail foot length. They shall be displayed wholly below an arc whose centre is the head point and whose radius is half the luff length and, if possible, wholly above an arc whose radius is 75% of the luff length.

**R⁄A G2    OTHER BOATS**

Other boats shall comply with the rules of their national authority or class association in regard to the allotment, carrying and size of insignia, letters and numbers. Such rules shall, when practicable, conform to the above requirements.

**G3    CHARTERED OR LOANED BOATS**

When so stated in the notice of race or sailing instructions, a boat chartered or loaned for an event may carry national letters or a sail number in contravention of her class rules.

**G4    WARNINGS AND PENALTIES**

When a protest committee finds that a boat has broken a rule of this appendix, it shall either warn her and give her time to comply or penalize her.

**G5    CHANGES BY CLASS RULES**

World Sailing Classes may change the rules of this appendix provided the changes have first been approved by World Sailing.

# APPENDIX H
# WEIGHING CLOTHING AND EQUIPMENT

*See rule 43. This appendix shall not be changed by sailing instructions or prescriptions of national authorities.*

**H1**    Items of clothing and equipment to be weighed shall be arranged on a rack. After being saturated in water the items shall be allowed to drain freely for one minute before being weighed. The rack must allow the items to hang as they would hang from clothes hangers, so as to allow the water to drain freely. Pockets that have drain-holes that cannot be closed shall be empty, but pockets or items that can hold water shall be full.

**H2**    When the weight recorded exceeds the amount permitted, the competitor may rearrange the items on the rack and the member of the technical committee in charge shall again soak and weigh them. This procedure may be repeated a second time if the weight still exceeds the amount permitted.

**H3**    A competitor wearing a dry suit may choose an alternative means of weighing the items

(a)    The dry suit and items of clothing and equipment that are worn outside the dry suit shall be weighed as described above.

(b)    Clothing worn underneath the dry suit shall be weighed as worn while *racing*, without draining.

(c)    The two weights shall be added together.

# APPENDIX J
# NOTICE OF RACE AND SAILING INSTRUCTIONS

*See rules 89.2 and 90.2. In this appendix, the term 'race' includes a regatta or other series of races.*

*Care should be taken to ensure that there is no conflict between a rule in the notice of race and a rule in the sailing instructions.*

**J1**  **NOTICE OF RACE CONTENTS**

**J1.1**  The notice of race shall include the following information:

(1)  the title, place and dates of the race and name of the organizing authority;

(2)  that the race will be governed by the *rules* as defined in *The Racing Rules of Sailing*;

(3)  a list of any other documents that will govern the event (for example, *The Equipment Rules of Sailing*, to the extent that they apply), stating where or how each document or a copy of it may be seen;

(4)  the classes to race, any handicap or rating system that will be used and the classes to which it will apply, conditions of entry and any restrictions on entries;

(5)  the times of registration and warning signals for the practice race, if one is scheduled, and the first race, and succeeding races if known.

**J1.2**  The notice of race shall include any of the following that will apply and that would help competitors decide whether to attend the event or that conveys other information they will need before the sailing instructions become available:

(1)  changes to the racing rules permitted by rule 86, referring specifically to each rule and stating the change (also, if rule 86.2 applies, include the statement from World Sailing authorizing the change);

(2)  that boats will be required to display advertising chosen and supplied by the organizing authority (see rule 80 and World Sailing Regulation 20, Advertising Code) and other information related to Regulation 20;

(3)    any classification requirements that some or all competitors must satisfy (see rule 79 and World Sailing Regulation 22, Sailor Classification Code);

(4)    for an event where entries from other countries are expected, any national prescriptions that may require advance preparation (see rule 88);

(5)    the procedures for registration or entry, including fees and any closing dates;

(6)    an entry form, to be signed by the boat's owner or owner's representative, containing words such as 'I agree to be bound by *The Racing Rules of Sailing* and by all other *rules* that govern this event.';

(7)    times or procedures for equipment inspection or event measurement, or requirements for measurement or rating certificates;

(8)    the time and place at which the sailing instructions will be available;

(9)    changes to class rules, as permitted under rule 87, referring specifically to each rule and stating the change;

(10)   the courses to be sailed;

(11)   the time after which no warning signal will be made on the last scheduled day of racing;

(12)   the penalty for breaking a rule of Part 2, other than the Two-Turns Penalty;

(13)   denial of the right of appeal, subject to rule 70.5;

(14)   the scoring system, if different from the Low Point System in Appendix A, included by reference to class rules or other *rules* governing the event. State the number of races scheduled and the minimum number that must be completed to constitute a series;

(15)   for chartered or loaned boats, whether rule G3 applies;

(16)   prizes.

## J2    SAILING INSTRUCTION CONTENTS

**J2.1**    The sailing instructions shall include the following information:

(1)    that the race will be governed by the *rules* as defined in *The Racing Rules of Sailing*;

(2)    a list of any other documents that will govern the event (for example, *The Equipment Rules of Sailing*, to the extent that they apply);

(3)    the schedule of races, the classes to race and times of warning signals for each class;

(4)    the course(s) to be sailed, or a list of *marks* from which the course will be selected and, if relevant, how courses will be signalled;

(5)    descriptions of *marks*, including starting and finishing *marks*, stating the order in which *marks* are to be passed and the side on which each is to be left and identifying all rounding *marks* (see rule 28.2);

(6)    descriptions of the starting and finishing lines, class flags and any special signals to be used;

(7)    the time limit, if any, for *finishing*;

(8)    the handicap or rating system to be used, if any, and the classes to which it will apply;

(9)    unless stated in the notice of race, the scoring system, if different from the Low Point System in Appendix A, included by reference to class rules or other *rules* governing the event, or stated in full. State the number of races scheduled and the minimum number that must be completed to constitute a series.

(10)    unless stated in the notice of race, location(s) of official notice board(s) or address of online notice board.

**J2.2**    The sailing instructions shall include those of the following that will apply:

(1)    that boats will be required to display advertising chosen and supplied by the organizing authority (see rule 80 and World Sailing Regulation 20, Advertising Code) and other information related to Regulation 20;

(2)    replacement of the rules of Part 2 with the right-of-way rules of the *International Regulations for Preventing Collisions at Sea* or other government right-of-way rules, the time(s) or place(s) they will apply, and any night signals to be used by the race committee;

(3)  changes to the racing rules permitted by rule 86, referring specifically to each rule and stating the change (also, if rule 86.2 applies, include the statement from World Sailing authorizing the change);

(4)  changes to the national prescriptions (see rule 88.2);

(5)  prescriptions that will apply if boats will pass through the waters of more than one national authority while *racing*, and when they will apply (see rule 88.1);

(6)  when appropriate, at an event where entries from other countries are expected, a copy in English of the national prescriptions that will apply;

(7)  changes to class rules, as permitted under rule 87, referring specifically to each rule and stating the change;

(8)  restrictions controlling changes to boats when supplied by the organizing authority;

(9)  unless included in the notice of race, times or procedures for equipment inspection or measurement;

(10)  procedure for changing the sailing instructions;

(11)  procedure for giving oral changes to the sailing instructions on the water (see rule 90.2(c));

(12)  safety requirements, such as requirements and signals for personal flotation devices, check-in at the starting area, and check-out and check-in ashore;

(13)  declaration requirements;

(14)  signals to be made ashore and location of signal station(s);

(15)  the racing area (a chart is recommended);

(16)  approximate course length and approximate length of windward legs;

(17)  description of any area designated by the race committee to be an *obstruction* (see the definition *Obstruction*);

(18)  the time after which no warning signal will be made on the last scheduled day of racing;

(19)  the time limit, if any, for the first boat to *finish* and the time limit, if any, for boats other than the first boat to *finish*;

(20) time allowances;

(21) location of the starting area and any restrictions on entering it;

(22) any special procedures or signals for individual or general recall;

(23) boats identifying *mark* locations;

(24) any special procedures or signals for changing a leg of the course (see rule 33);

(25) any special procedures for shortening the course or for *finishing* a shortened course;

(26) restrictions on use of support boats, plastic pools, radios, etc.; on trash disposal; on hauling out; and on outside assistance provided to a boat that is not *racing*;

(27) the penalty for breaking a rule of Part 2, other than the Two-Turns Penalty;

(28) whether Appendix P will apply;

(29) when and under what circumstances propulsion is permitted under rule 42.3(i);

(30) time limits, place of hearings, and special procedures for *protests*, requests for redress or requests for reopening;

(31) if rule N1.4(b) will apply, the time limit for requesting a hearing under that rule;

(32) denial of the right of appeal, subject to rule 70.5;

(33) when required by rule 70.3, the national authority to which appeals and requests may be sent;

(34) the national authority's approval of the appointment of an international jury, when required under rule 91(b);

(35) substitution of competitors;

(36) the minimum number of boats appearing in the starting area required for a race to be started;

(37) when and where races *postponed* or *abandoned* for the day will be sailed;

(38) tides and currents;

(39) prizes;

(40) other commitments of the race committee and obligations of boats.

## ADDENDUM A (RYA)

*The RYA recommends that paragraph 20 (Disclaimer of Liability) of Appendix K and paragraph 29 (Disclaimer of Liability) of Appendix L each are replaced with an appropriate "Risk Statement". An example Risk Statement is set out below. This Addendum also includes additional clauses that are recommended for inclusion in the Notice of Race.*

*Before using these clauses, race organisers are recommended to: conduct a risk assessment for the event; consider whether appropriate safety measures have been taken; consider whether competitors' attention needs to be drawn to any specific rules and information (e.g. by preparing a safety plan for the event and referencing this in the Sailing Instructions) and consider whether the suggested clauses are right for the event or need to be modified. The RYA provides guidance on the legal aspects of race, training and event management which is available to affiliated clubs, recognised training centres and members.*

*It is possible that, for some events, a more comprehensive set of race terms and conditions than those set out in the model Notice of Race in Appendix K and in this Addendum would be appropriate. Such race terms and conditions are outside the scope of this Addendum.*

### RISK STATEMENT

Rule 4 of the Racing Rules of Sailing states: "The responsibility for a boat's decision to participate in a race or to continue racing is hers alone."

Sailing is by its nature an unpredictable sport and therefore inherently involves an element of risk. By taking part in the event, each competitor agrees and acknowledges that:

(a)    They are aware of the inherent element of risk involved in the sport and accept responsibility for the exposure of themselves, their crew and their boat to such inherent risk whilst taking part in the event;

(b)    They are responsible for the safety of themselves, their crew, their boat and their other property whether afloat or ashore;

(c)    They accept responsibility for any injury, damage or loss to the extent caused by their own actions or omissions;

(d)    Their boat is in good order, equipped to sail in the event and they are fit to participate;

(e)    The provision of a race management team, patrol boats and other officials and volunteers by the event organiser does not relieve them of their own responsibilities;

(f)    The provision of patrol boat cover is limited to such assistance, particularly in extreme weather conditions, as can be practically provided in the circumstances;

(g)    It is their responsibility to familiarise themselves with any risks specific to this venue or this event drawn to their attention in any rules and information produced for the venue or event and to attend any safety briefing held for the event;

(h)    [[*For offshore races*] They are responsible for ensuring that their boat is equipped and seaworthy so as to be able to face extremes of weather; that there is a crew sufficient in number, experience and fitness to withstand such weather; and that the safety equipment is properly maintained, stowed and in date and is familiar to the crew]; and

(i)    [[*If not covered elsewhere in the Notice of Race*] Their boat is adequately insured, with cover of at least [£#] against third party claims].

## INSPECTIONS

The fact that race officials may conduct inspections of a boat does not reduce the responsibilities of each competitor set out in this Notice of Race.

## DECLARATION

*(To be contained in the entry form immediately above the signature of the competitor)*

I agree to be bound by the Racing Rules of Sailing and all other rules that govern this event. In particular, I confirm that I have read the Notice of Race and accept its provisions and agree that my boat will conform to the requirements set out in the Notice of Race throughout the event.

# APPENDIX K
# NOTICE OF RACE GUIDE

*This guide provides a notice of race designed primarily for major championship regattas for one or more classes. It therefore will be particularly useful for world, continental and national championships and other events of similar importance. It can be downloaded from the World Sailing website as a basic text for producing a notice of race for any particular event.*

*The guide can also be useful for other events. However, for such events some of the paragraphs will be unnecessary or undesirable. Organizing authorities should therefore be careful in making their choices.*

*This guide relates closely to Appendix L, Sailing Instructions Guide, and its expanded version Appendix LE on the World Sailing website, the introduction to which contains principles that also apply to a notice of race.*

*Rule references within the notice of race use RRS, NoR and SI to denote the source of the rule. 'RRS x' is a rule in* The Racing Rules of Sailing. *'NoR x' is a rule in the notice of race, and 'SI x' is a rule in the sailing instructions.*

*To use this guide, first review rule J1 and decide which paragraphs will be needed. Paragraphs that are required by rule J1.1 are marked with an asterisk (\*). Delete all inapplicable or unnecessary paragraphs. Select the version preferred where there is a choice. Follow the directions in the left margin to fill in the spaces where a solid line ( _____ ) appears and select the preferred wording if a choice or option is shown in brackets ([ . . . ]).*

*After deleting unused paragraphs, renumber all paragraphs in sequential order. Be sure that paragraph numbers are correct where one paragraph refers to another.*

*Care should be taken to ensure that there is no conflict between a rule in the notice of race and a rule in the sailing instructions.*

*If the notice of race is made available electronically, printed copies should be provided on request.*

*The items listed below, when applicable, should be distributed with the notice of race, but should not be included as numbered paragraphs in the notice.*

1   *An entry form, to be signed by the boat's owner or owner's representative, containing words such as 'I agree to be bound by* The Racing Rules of Sailing *and by all other rules that govern this event.'*

2   *For an event where entries from other countries are expected, the applicable national prescriptions in English.*

3   *List of sponsors, if appropriate.*

4   *Lodging and camping information.*

5   *Description of meal facilities.*

6   *Race committee and protest committee members.*

7   *Special mooring or storage requirements.*

8   *Sail and boat repair facilities and ship's chandlers.*

9   *Availability of chartered or loaned boats and whether rule G3 will apply.*

*On separate lines, insert the full name of the regatta, the inclusive dates from equipment inspection, event measurement or the practice race until the final race or closing ceremony, the name of the organizing authority, and the city and country.*

_____

_____

_____

_____

## NOTICE OF RACE

*The notation '[DP]' in a rule in the NoR means that the penalty for a breach of that rule may, at the discretion of the protest committee, be less than disqualification.*

### 1    RULES

**1.1\***   The regatta will be governed by the rules as defined in *The Racing Rules of Sailing*.

*Use the first sentence if appropriate. Insert the name. List by number and title the prescriptions that will not apply (see RRS 88). Use the second sentence if it applies and if entries from other countries are expected, and state the relevant prescriptions in full.*

**1.2** [The following prescriptions of the _____ national authority will not apply: _____.] [The prescriptions that may require advance preparation are stated in full below.]

**(OR)**

*Use if appropriate, but only if the national authority for the venue of the event has not adopted a prescription to RRS 88.*

**1.2** No national prescriptions will apply.

*List by name any other documents that govern the event; for example, The Equipment Rules of Sailing, to the extent that they apply.*

**1.3\*** _____ will apply.

*See RRS 86. Insert the rule number(s) and summarize the changes.*

**1.4** Racing rule(s) _____ will be changed as follows: _____. The changes will appear in full in the sailing instructions. The sailing instructions may also change other racing rules.

**(OR)**

*See RRS 86. Either insert here the rule number(s) and state the changes, or, if not using this NoR, do the same in each NoR that changes a racing rule.*

**1.4** Racing rule(s) _____ will be changed as follows: _____.

*Insert the rule number(s) and class name. Make a separate statement for the rules of each class.*

**1.5** Under RRS 87, rule(s) _____ of the _____ class rules [will not apply] [is (are) changed as follows: _____ ].

141

**1.6** If there is a conflict between languages the English text will take precedence.

*Use only if RRS Appendix S, Standard Sailing Instructions, will be used.*

*Insert the location.*

**1.7** The sailing instructions will consist of the instructions in RRS Appendix S, Standard Sailing Instructions, and supplementary sailing instructions that will be on the official notice board located at _____.

## 2   ADVERTISING

*See World Sailing Regulation 20, Advertising Code. Include other applicable information related to Regulation 20.*

**2.1** Competitor advertising will be restricted as follows: _____.

*See World Sailing Regulation 20.4.*

**2.2** Boats [shall] [may be required to] display advertising chosen and supplied by the organizing authority. If this rule is broken, World Sailing Regulation 20.9.2 applies. [DP] .

## 3*   ELIGIBILITY AND ENTRY

*Insert the class(es).*

**3.1** The regatta is open to all boats of the _____ class(es).

**(OR)**

*Insert the class(es) and eligibility requirements.*

**3.1** The regatta is open to boats of the _____ class(es) that _____.

*Insert the postal, fax and email addresses and entry closing date.*

**3.2** Eligible boats may enter by completing the attached form and sending it, together with the required fee, to _____ by _____.

*Insert any conditions.*

**3.3** Late entries will be accepted under the following conditions: _____.

*Insert any restrictions.*

**3.4** The following restrictions on the number of boats apply: _____.

**4     CLASSIFICATION**

*Insert any requirements.*

The following classification requirements will apply (see RRS 79): _____.

**5     FEES**

*Insert all required fees for racing.*

**5.1**   Required fees are as follows:

| Class | Fee |
|-------|-----|
| _____ | _____ |
| _____ | _____ |
| _____ | _____ |

*Insert optional fees (for example, for social events).*

**5.2**   Other fees:

_____

_____

**6     QUALIFYING SERIES AND FINAL SERIES**

*Use only when a class is divided into fleets racing a qualifying series and a final series.*

The regatta will consist of a qualifying series and a final series.

**7     SCHEDULE**

**7.1***  Registration:

*Insert the day, date and times.*

Day and date _____
From _____          To _____

**7.2**   Equipment inspection and event measurement:

*Insert the day, date and times.*

Day and date _____
From _____          To _____

*Revise as desired and insert the dates and classes. Include a practice race if any. When the series consists of qualifying races and final races, specify them. The schedule can also be given in an attachment.*

**7.3\*** Dates of racing:

| Date | Class _____ | Class _____ |
|------|-------------|-------------|
| _____ | racing | racing |
| _____ | racing | reserve day |
| _____ | reserve day | racing |
| _____ | racing | racing |
| _____ | racing | racing |

*Insert the classes and numbers.*

**7.4** Number of races:

| Class | Number | Races per day |
|-------|--------|---------------|
| _____ | _____ | _____ |
| _____ | _____ | _____ |

*Insert the time.*

**7.5\*** The scheduled time of the warning signal for the [practice race] [first race] [each day] is _____.

*Use when it would be helpful to competitors to know this time before the event. Insert the time.*

**7.6** On the last scheduled day of racing no warning signal will be made after _____.

**8    MEASUREMENT**

**8.1** Each boat shall produce a valid [measurement] [rating] certificate.

**(OR)**

**8.1** Each boat shall produce a valid [measurement] [rating] certificate. In addition the following equipment [may] [will] be inspected or measured: _____.

*List the equipment with appropriate references to the class rules.*

**8.2** A boat shall comply with RRS 78.1 at _____.

*Insert the time(s).*

**9    SAILING INSTRUCTIONS**

*Insert the time, date and location.*

The sailing instructions will be available after _____ on _____ at _____.

## 10    VENUE

*Insert a number or letter. Provide a marked map with driving instructions.*

**10.1**    Attachment _____ shows the location of the regatta harbour.

*Insert a number or letter. Provide a marked map or chart.*

**10.2**    Attachment _____ shows the location of the racing areas.

## 11    THE COURSES

The courses to be sailed will be as follows: _____.

*Include the description.*

**(OR)**

*Insert a number or letter. A method of illustrating various courses is shown in Addendum A of Appendix L or LE. Insert the course length if applicable.*

The diagrams in Attachment _____ show the courses, including the approximate angles between legs, the order in which marks are to be passed, and the side on which each mark is to be left. [The approximate course length will be_____.]

## 12    PENALTY SYSTEM

*Include paragraph 12.1 only when the Two-Turns Penalty will not be used. Insert the number of places or describe the penalties.*

**12.1**    The Scoring Penalty, RRS 44.3, will apply. The penalty will be _____ places.

**(OR)**

**12.1**    The penalties are as follows: _____.

*Insert the class(es).*

**12.2**    For the _____ class(es) RRS 44.1 is changed so that the Two-Turns Penalty is replaced by the One-Turn Penalty.

*Include only if the protest committee is an international jury or another provision of RRS 70.5 applies.*

**12.3**    Decisions of the [protest committee] [international jury] will be final as provided in RRS 70.5.

## 13     SCORING

*Include only if the Low Point System of Appendix A will not be used. Describe the system.*

**13.1**     The scoring system is as follows: _____.

*Insert the number.*

**13.2**     _____ races are required to be completed to constitute a series.

*Insert the numbers throughout.*

**13.3**     (a)  When fewer than _____ races have been completed, a boat's series score will be the total of her race scores.

(b)  When from _____ to _____ races have been completed, a boat's series score will be the total of her race scores excluding her worst score.

(c)  When _____ or more races have been completed, a boat's series score will be the total of her race scores excluding her two worst scores.

## 14     SUPPORT BOATS

*Insert the identification markings. National letters are suggested for international events.*

Support boats shall be marked with _____. [DP]

## 15     BERTHING

Boats shall be kept in their assigned places while they are in the [boat park] [harbour]. [DP]

## 16     HAUL-OUT RESTRICTIONS

Keelboats shall not be hauled out during the regatta except with and according to the terms of prior written permission of the race committee. [DP]

### 17    DIVING EQUIPMENT AND PLASTIC POOLS

Underwater breathing apparatus and plastic pools or their equivalent shall not be used around keelboats between the preparatory signal of the first race and the end of the regatta. [DP]

### 18    RADIO COMMUNICATION

*Insert any alternative text that applies. Describe any radio communication bands or frequencies that will be used or allowed.*

Except in an emergency, a boat that is racing shall not make voice or data transmissions and shall not receive voice or data communication that is not available to all boats. [DP]

### 19    PRIZES

*If perpetual trophies will be awarded state their complete names.*

Prizes will be given as follows: _____.

### 20    DISCLAIMER OF LIABILITY

*The laws applicable to the venue in which the event is held may limit disclaimers. Any disclaimer should be drafted to comply with those laws.*

Competitors participate in the regatta entirely at their own risk. See RRS 4, Decision to Race. The organizing authority will not accept any liability for material damage or personal injury or death sustained in conjunction with or prior to, during, or after the regatta.

### 21    INSURANCE

*Insert the currency and amount.*

Each participating boat shall be insured with valid third-party liability insurance with a minimum cover of _____ per incident or the equivalent.

### 22    FURTHER INFORMATION

*Insert necessary contact information.*

For further information please contact _____.

# APPENDIX L
# SAILING INSTRUCTIONS GUIDE

*This guide provides a set of tested sailing instructions designed primarily for major championship regattas for one or more classes. It therefore will be particularly useful for world, continental and national championships and other events of similar importance. The guide can also be useful for other events; however, for such events some of these instructions will be unnecessary or undesirable. Race officers should therefore be careful in making their choices.*

*An expanded version of the guide, Appendix LE, is available on the World Sailing website. It contains provisions applicable to the largest and most complicated multi-class events, as well as variations on several of the sailing instructions recommended in this appendix. It will be revised from time to time, to reflect advances in race management techniques as they develop, and can be downloaded as a basic text for producing the sailing instructions for any particular event. Appendix L can also be downloaded from the World Sailing website.*

*The principles on which all sailing instructions should be based are as follows:*

1   *They should include only two types of statement: the intentions of the race committee and protest committee and the obligations of competitors.*

2   *They should be concerned only with racing. Information about social events, assignment of moorings, etc., should be provided separately.*

3   *They should not change the racing rules except when clearly desirable. (When they do so, they must follow rule 86 by referring specifically to the rule being changed and stating the change.)*

4   *They should not repeat or restate any of the racing rules.*

5   *They should not repeat themselves.*

6   *They should be in chronological order; that is, the order in which the competitor will use them.*

7   *They should, when possible, use words or phrases from the racing rules.*

*Rule references within the sailing instructions use RRS, SI and NoR to denote the source of the rule. 'RRS x' is a rule in* The Racing Rules of Sailing. *'SI x' is a rule in the sailing instructions, and 'NoR x' is a rule in the notice of race.*

*To use this guide, first review rule J2 and decide which instructions will be needed. Instructions that are required by rule J2.1 are marked with an asterisk (\*). Delete all inapplicable or unnecessary instructions. Select the version preferred where there is a choice. Follow the directions in the left margin to fill in the spaces where a solid line ( _____ ) appears and select the preferred wording if a choice or option is shown in brackets ([ . . . ]).*

*After deleting unused instructions, renumber all instructions in sequential order. Be sure that instruction numbers are correct where one instruction refers to another.*

*Care should be taken to ensure that there is no conflict between a rule in the notice of race and a rule in the sailing instructions.*

*If the sailing instructions are made available electronically, printed copies should be provided on request.*

*On separate lines, insert the full name of the regatta, the inclusive dates from equipment inspection, event measurement or the practice race until the final race or closing ceremony, the name of the organizing authority, and the city and country.*

_____

_____

_____

_____

## SAILING INSTRUCTIONS

The notation '[DP]' in a rule in the SI means that the penalty for a breach of that rule may, at the discretion of the protest committee, be less than disqualification.

**1    RULES**

**1.1\***    The regatta will be governed by the rules as defined in *The Racing Rules of Sailing.*

*Use the first sentence if appropriate. Insert the name. List by number and title the prescriptions that will not apply (see RRS 88.2). Use the second sentence if it applies and if entries from other national authorities are expected, and state the prescriptions in full. Include the prescriptions in English when appropriate (see RRS 90.2(b)).*

**1.2**  [The following prescriptions of the _____ national authority will not apply: _____.] [The prescriptions that will apply are stated in full below.]

**(OR)**

*Use if appropriate, but only if the national authority for the venue of the event has not adopted a prescription to RRS 88.*

**1.2**  No national prescriptions will apply.

*List by name any other documents that govern the event; for example, The Equipment Rules of Sailing, to the extent that they apply.*

**1.3\***  _____ will apply.

*See RRS 86. Either insert here the rule number(s) and state the changes, or, if not using this instruction, do the same in each instruction that changes a racing rule.*

**1.4**  Racing rule(s) _____ will be changed as follows: _____.

*Insert the rule number(s) and class name. Make a separate statement for the rules of each class.*

**1.5**  Under RRS 87, rule(s) _____ of the _____ class rules [will not apply] [is (are) changed as follows: _____].

**1.6**  If there is a conflict between languages the English text will take precedence.

*Insert the location(s). If notices are online, state how and where they may be found.*

**2\*    NOTICES TO COMPETITORS**

Notices to competitors will be posted on the official notice board(s) located at ____.

**3    CHANGES TO SAILING INSTRUCTIONS**

*Change the times if different.*

Any change to the sailing instructions will be posted before 0900 on the day it will take effect, except that any change to the schedule of races will be posted by 2000 on the day before it will take effect.

**4    SIGNALS MADE ASHORE**

*Insert the location.*

**4.1**    Signals made ashore will be displayed at ____.

*Insert the number of minutes.*

**4.2**    When flag AP is displayed ashore, '1 minute' is replaced with 'not less than ____ minutes' in the race signal AP.

**(OR)**

*Insert the number of minutes.*

**4.2**    Flag D with one sound means 'The warning signal will be made not less than ____ minutes after flag D is displayed. [Boats are requested not to leave the harbour until this signal is made.] [Boats shall not leave the harbour until this signal is made. [DP]]'

**5    SCHEDULE OF RACES**

*Revise as desired and insert the dates and classes. Include a practice race if any. When the series consists of qualifying races and final races, specify them. The schedule can also be given in an attachment.*

**5.1\***    Dates of racing:

| Date | Class ____ | Class ____ |
|------|------------|------------|
| ____ | racing | racing |
| ____ | racing | reserve day |
| ____ | reserve day | racing |
| ____ | racing | racing |
| ____ | racing | racing |

**5.2**   Number of races:

*Insert the classes and numbers.*

| Class | Number | Races per day |
|-------|--------|---------------|
| _____ | _____  | _____         |
| _____ | _____  | _____         |

One extra race per day may be sailed, provided that no class becomes more than one race ahead of schedule and the change is made according to SI 3.l

*Insert the time.*   **5.3\***   The scheduled time of the warning signal for the first race each day is _____.

**5.4**   To alert boats that a race or sequence of races will begin soon, the orange starting line flag will be displayed with one sound at least five minutes before a warning signal is made.

*Insert the time.*   **5.5**   On the last scheduled day of racing no warning signal will be made after _____.

**6\***   **CLASS FLAGS**

*Insert the classes and names or descriptions of the flags.*

Class flags will be:

| Class | Flag  |
|-------|-------|
| _____ | _____ |
| _____ | _____ |
| _____ | _____ |

**7**   **RACING AREAS**

*Insert a number or letter.*   Attachment _____ shows the location of racing areas.

**8**   **THE COURSES**

*Insert a number or letter. A method of illustrating various courses is shown in Addendum A. Insert the course length if applicable.*

**8.1\***   The diagrams in Attachment _____ show the courses, including the approximate angles between legs, the order in which marks are to be passed, and the side on which each mark is to be left. [The approximate course length will be _____.]

**8.2** No later than the warning signal, the race committee signal vessel will display the approximate compass bearing of the first leg.

**8.3** Courses will not be shortened. This changes RRS 32.

*Include only when changing positions of marks is impracticable.*

**8.4** Legs of the course will not be changed after the preparatory signal. This changes RRS 33.

**9** **MARKS**

*Change the mark numbers as needed and insert the descriptions of the marks. Use the second alternative when Marks 4S and 4P form a gate, with Mark 4S to be left to starboard and Mark 4P to port.*

**9.1\*** Marks 1, 2, 3 and 4 will be _____.

**(OR)**

**9.1\*** Marks 1, 2, 3, 4S and 4P will be _____.

**(OR)**

*Insert the number or letter used in SI 8.1.*

**9.1\*** Marks are described in Attachment _____.

*Unless it is clear from the course diagrams, list the marks that are rounding marks.*

**9.2** The following marks are rounding marks:

_____.

*Insert the descriptions of the marks.*

**9.3** New marks, as provided in SI 12.1, will be

_____.

*Describe the starting and finishing marks: for example, the race committee signal vessel at the starboard end and a buoy at the port end. SI 11.2 will describe the starting line and SI 13 the finishing line.*

**9.4\*** The starting and finishing marks will be ____.

*Include if SI 12.2 is included.*

**9.5** A race committee vessel signalling a change of a leg of the course is a mark as provided in SI 12.2.

*Describe each area by its location and any easily recognized details of appearance.*

**10** **AREAS THAT ARE OBSTRUCTIONS**
The following areas are designated as obstructions: ____.

**11** **THE START**

*Include only if the asterisked option in RRS 26 will be used. Insert the number of minutes.*

**11.1** Races will be started by using RRS 26 with the warning signal made ____ minutes before the starting signal.

**(OR)**

*Describe any starting system other than that stated in RRS 26.*

**11.1** Races will be started as follows: ____. This changes RRS 26.

**11.2\*** The starting line will be between staffs displaying orange flags on the starting marks.

**(OR)**

**11.2\*** The starting line will be between a staff displaying an orange flag on the starting mark at the starboard end and the course side of the port-end starting mark.

**(OR)**

*Insert the description.*

**11.2\*** The starting line will be ____.

**11.3** Boats whose warning signal has not been made shall avoid the starting area during the starting sequence for other races. [DP]

*Insert the number of minutes.*

**11.4** A boat that does not start within _____ minutes after her starting signal will be scored Did Not Start without a hearing. This changes RRS A4 and A5.

*Insert the channel number.*

**11.5** If any part of a boat's hull, crew or equipment is on the course side of the starting line during the two minutes before her starting signal and she is identified, the race committee will attempt to broadcast her sail number on VHF channel _____. Failure to make a broadcast or to time it accurately will not be grounds for a request for redress. This changes RRS 62.1(a).

## 12    CHANGE OF THE NEXT LEG OF THE COURSE

**12.1** To change the next leg of the course, the race committee will move the original mark (or the finishing line) to a new position.

**(OR)**

**12.1** To change the next leg of the course, the race committee will lay a new mark (or move the finishing line) and remove the original mark as soon as practicable. When in a subsequent change a new mark is replaced, it will be replaced by an original mark.

*When SI 12.2 is included, SI 9.5 must also be included. Reverse 'port' and 'starboard' when the mark is to be left to starboard.*

**12.2** Except at a gate, boats shall pass between the race committee vessel signalling the change of the next leg and the nearby mark, leaving the mark to port and the race committee vessel to starboard. This changes RRS 28.

## 13    THE FINISH

**13.1*** The finishing line will be between staffs displaying orange flags on the finishing marks.

**(OR)**

**13.1*** The finishing line will be between a staff displaying an orange flag on the finishing mark at the starboard end and the course side of the port-end finishing mark.

**(OR)**

*Insert the description.*

**13.1*** The finishing line will be _____.

**13.2** If the race committee is absent when a boat finishes, she should report her finishing time, and her position in relation to nearby boats, to the race committee at the first reasonable opportunity.

## 14    PENALTY SYSTEM

*Include SI 14.1 only when the Two-Turns Penalty will not be used. Insert the number of places or describe the penalties.*

**14.1** The Scoring Penalty, RRS 44.3, will apply. The penalty will be _____ places.

**(OR)**

**14.1** The penalties are as follows: _____.

*Insert the class(es).*

**14.2** For the _____ class(es) RRS 44.1 is changed so that the Two-Turns Penalty is replaced by the One-Turn Penalty.

*Unless all of Appendix P applies, state any restrictions.*

**14.3** Appendix P will apply [as changed by SI(s) [14.2] [and] [14.4]].

*Recommended only for junior events.*

**14.4** RRS P2.3 will not apply and RRS P2.2 is changed so that it will apply to any penalty after the first one.

## 15    TIME LIMITS AND TARGET TIMES

*Insert the classes and times. Omit the Mark 1 time limit and target time if inapplicable.*

**15.1\***  Time limits and target times are as follows:

| Class | Time limit | Mark 1 time limit | Target time |
|-------|-----------|-------------------|-------------|
| _____ | _____ | _____ | _____ |
| _____ | _____ | _____ | _____ |
| _____ | _____ | _____ | _____ |

If no boat has passed Mark 1 within the Mark 1 time limit the race will be abandoned. Failure to meet the target time will not be grounds for redress. This changes RRS 62.1(a).

*Insert the time (or different times for different classes).*

**15.2**  Boats failing to finish within _____ after the first boat sails the course and finishes will be scored Did Not Finish without a hearing. This changes RRS 35, A4 and A5.

## 16    PROTESTS AND REQUESTS FOR REDRESS

*State the location if necessary.*

**16.1**  Protest forms are available at the race office[, located at _____]. Protests and requests for redress or reopening shall be delivered there within the appropriate time limit.

*Change the time if different.*

**16.2**  For each class, the protest time limit is 90 minutes after the last boat has finished the last race of the day or the race committee signals no more racing today, whichever is later.

*Change the posting time if different. Insert the protest room location and, if applicable, the time for the first hearing.*

**16.3**  Notices will be posted no later than 30 minutes after the protest time limit to inform competitors of hearings in which they are parties or named as witnesses. Hearings will be held in the protest room, located at _____, beginning at [the time posted] [_____].

**16.4**  Notices of protests by the race committee, technical committee or protest committee will be posted to inform boats under RRS 61.1(b).

**16.5**  A list of boats that, under SI 14.3, have been penalized for breaking RRS 42 will be posted.

**16.6**  Breaches of SIs 11.3, 18, 21, 23, 25, 26 and 27 will not be grounds for a protest by a boat. This changes RRS 60.1(a).

**16.7**  On the last scheduled day of racing a request for redress based on a protest committee decision shall be delivered no later than 30 minutes after the decision was posted. This changes RRS 62.2.

*Include only if RRS 70.5 applies.*

**16.8**  Decisions of the [protest committee] [international jury] will be final as provided in RRS 70.5.

## 17    SCORING

*Include only if the Low Point System of Appendix A will not be used. Describe the system.*

**17.1**  The scoring system is as follows: _____.

*Insert the number.*

**17.2**  _____ races are required to be completed to constitute a series.

*Insert the numbers throughout.*

**17.3**  (a) When fewer than _____ races have been completed, a boat's series score will be the total of her race scores.

(b) When from _____ to _____ races have been completed, a boat's series score will be the total of her race scores excluding her worst score.

(c) When _____ or more races have been completed, a boat's series score will be the total of her race scores excluding her two worst scores.

## 18    SAFETY REGULATIONS

*Insert the procedure for check-out and check-in.*

**18.1**    Check-Out and Check-In: _____. [DP]

**18.2**    A boat that retires from a race shall notify the race committee as soon as possible. [DP]

## 19    REPLACEMENT OF CREW OR EQUIPMENT

**19.1**    Substitution of competitors will not be allowed without prior written approval of the [race committee] [protest committee]. [DP]

**19.2**    Substitution of damaged or lost equipment will not be allowed unless authorized by the [race committee] [protest committee]. Requests for substitution shall be made to the committee at the first reasonable opportunity. [DP]

## 20    EQUIPMENT AND MEASUREMENT CHECKS

On the water, a boat can be instructed by a member of the race committee or the technical committee to proceed immediately to a designated area for inspection. Ashore, equipment may be inspected or measured at times specified in the class rules, the notice of race, and at the following time(s) _____.

*Insert the time(s).*

## 21    EVENT ADVERTISING

*See World Sailing Regulation 20.4. Insert necessary information on the display of event advertising material.*

Boats shall display event advertising supplied by the organizing authority as follows: _____. If this rule is broken, World Sailing Regulation 20.9.2 applies. [DP]

## 22    OFFICIAL BOATS

*Insert the descriptions. If appropriate, use different identification markings for boats performing different duties.*

Official boats will be marked as follows: _____.

## 23    SUPPORT BOATS

**23.1**  Team leaders, coaches and other support persons shall stay outside areas where boats are racing from the time of the preparatory signal for the first class to start until all boats have finished or retired or the race committee signals a postponement, general recall or abandonment. [DP]

*Insert the identification markings. National letters are suggested for international events.*

**23.2**  Support boats shall be marked with _____. [DP]

## 24    TRASH DISPOSAL

Trash may be placed aboard support or official boats.

## 25    HAUL-OUT RESTRICTIONS

Keelboats shall not be hauled out during the regatta except with and according to the terms of prior written permission of the race committee. [DP]

### 26    DIVING EQUIPMENT AND PLASTIC POOLS

Underwater breathing apparatus and plastic pools or their equivalent shall not be used around keelboats between the preparatory signal of the first race and the end of the regatta. [DP]

### 27    RADIO COMMUNICATION

*Insert any alternative text that applies. Describe any radio communication bands or frequencies that will be used or allowed.*

Except in an emergency, a boat that is racing shall not make voice or data transmissions and shall not receive voice or data communication that is not available to all boats. [DP]

### 28    PRIZES

*If perpetual trophies will be awarded state their complete names.*

Prizes will be given as follows: _____.

### 29    DISCLAIMER OF LIABILITY

*The laws applicable to the venue in which the event is held may limit disclaimers. Any disclaimer should be drafted to comply with those laws.*

Competitors participate in the regatta entirely at their own risk. See RRS 4, Decision to Race. The organizing authority will not accept any liability for material damage or personal injury or death sustained in conjunction with or prior to, during, or after the regatta.

### 30    INSURANCE

*Insert the currency and amount.*

Each participating boat shall be insured with valid third-party liability insurance with a minimum cover of _____ per incident or the equivalent.

## ADDENDUM A
# ILLUSTRATING THE COURSE

*Shown here are diagrams of course shapes. The boat's track is represented by a discontinuous line so that each diagram can describe courses with different numbers of laps. If more than one course may be used for a class, state how each particular course will be signalled.*

### A Windward-Leeward Course

**Start – 1 – 2 – 1 – 2 – Finish**

*Options for this course include*
*(1)    increasing or decreasing the number of laps,*
*(2)    deleting the last windward leg,*
*(3)    using a gate instead of a leeward mark,*
*(4)    using an offset mark at the windward mark, and*
*(5)    using the leeward and windward marks as starting and finishing marks.*

## A Triangle-Windward-Leeward Course

### Start – 1 – 2 – 3 – 1 – 3 – Finish

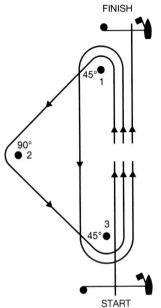

*Options for this course include*

(1) *increasing or decreasing the number of laps,*
(2) *deleting the last windward leg,*
(3) *varying the interior angles of the triangle (45°–90°–45° and 60°–60°–60° are common),*
(4) *using a gate instead of a leeward mark for downwind legs,*
(5) *using an offset mark at the beginning of downwind legs, and*
(6) *using the leeward and windward marks as starting and finishing marks.*

*Be sure to specify the interior angle at each mark.*

## Trapezoid Courses

**Start – 1 – 2 – 3 – 2 – 3 – Finish**       **Start – 1 – 4 – 1 – 2 – 3 – Finish**

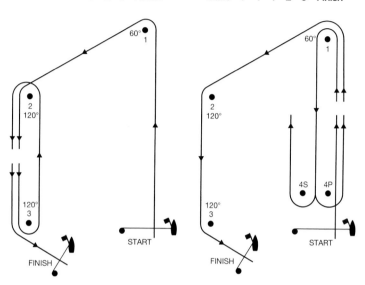

Options for this course include

(1)   adding additional legs,
(2)   replacing the gate shown by a single mark, or using a gate also in the outer loop,
(3)   varying the interior angles of the reaching legs,
(4)   using an offset mark at the beginning of downwind legs, and
(5)   finishing boats upwind rather than on a reach.

Be sure to specify the interior angle of each reaching leg.

## ADDENDUM B
# BOATS PROVIDED BY THE ORGANIZING AUTHORITY

*The following sailing instruction is recommended when all boats will be provided by the organizing authority. It can be changed to suit the circumstances. When used, it should be inserted after SI 3.*

**4      BOATS**

**4.1**    Boats will be provided for all competitors, who shall not modify them or cause them to be modified in any way except that

    (a)    a compass may be tied or taped to the hull or spars;

    (b)    wind indicators, including yarn or thread, may be tied or taped anywhere on the boat;

    (c)    hulls, centreboards and rudders may be cleaned, but only with water;

    (d)    adhesive tape may be used anywhere above the water line; and

    (e)    all fittings or equipment designed to be adjusted may be adjusted, provided that the class rules are complied with.

**4.2**    All equipment provided with the boat for sailing purposes shall be in the boat while afloat.

**4.3**    The penalty for not complying with one of the above instructions will be disqualification from all races sailed in which the instruction was broken.

**4.4**    Competitors shall report any damage or loss of equipment, however slight, to the organizing authority's representative immediately after securing the boat ashore. The penalty for breaking this instruction, unless the protest committee is satisfied that the competitor made a determined effort to comply, will be disqualification from the race most recently sailed.

**4.5**    Class rules requiring competitors to be members of the class association will not apply.

# APPENDIX M
## RECOMMENDATIONS FOR PROTEST COMMITTEES

*This appendix is advisory only; in some circumstances changing these procedures may be advisable. It is addressed primarily to protest committee chairmen but may also help judges, protest committee secretaries, race committees and others connected with protest and redress hearings.*

In a protest or redress hearing, the protest committee should weigh all testimony with equal care; should recognize that honest testimony can vary, and even be in conflict, as a result of different observations and recollections; should resolve such differences as best it can; should recognize that no boat or competitor is guilty until a breach of a *rule* has been established to the satisfaction of the protest committee; and should keep an open mind until all the evidence has been heard as to whether a boat or competitor has broken a *rule*.

**M1 PRELIMINARIES (may be performed by race office staff)**

- Receive the *protest* or request for redress.

- Note on the form the time the *protest* or request is delivered and the protest time limit.

- Inform each *party*, and the race committee when necessary, when and where the hearing will be held.

**M2 BEFORE THE HEARING**

**M2.1** Make sure that:

- each *party* has a copy of or the opportunity to read the *protest* or request for redress and has had reasonable time to prepare for the hearing;

- only one person from each boat (or *party*) is present unless an interpreter is needed;

- all boats and people involved are represented. If they are not, however, the committee may proceed under rule 63.3(b);

- boats' representatives were on board when required (rule 63.3(a)). When the *parties* were in different races, both organizing authorities must accept the composition of the protest committee (rule 63.8). In a *protest* concerning class rules, obtain the current class rules and identify the authority responsible for interpreting them (rule 64.3(b)).

**M2.2**   Determine if any members of the protest committee saw the incident. If so, require each of them to state that fact in the presence of the *parties* (rule 63.6).

**M2.3**   Assess *conflicts of interest.*

- Ensure that all protest committee members declare any possible *conflicts of interest*. At major events this will often be a formal written declaration made before the event starts that will be kept with the protest committee records.

- At the start of any hearing, ensure that the *parties* are aware of any *conflicts of interest* of protest committee members. Ask the *parties* if they consent to the members. If a *party* does not object as soon as possible after a *conflict of interest* has been declared, the protest committee may take this as consent to proceed and should record it.

- If a *party* objects to a member, the remainder of the protest committee members need to assess whether the *conflict of interest* is significant. The assessment will consider the level of the event, the level of the conflict and the perception of fairness. It may be acceptable to balance conflicts between protest committee members. Guidance may be found on the World Sailing website. Record the decision and the grounds for that decision.

- In cases of doubt it may be preferable to proceed with a smaller protest committee. Except for hearings under rule 69, there is no minimum number of protest committee members required.

- When a request for redress is made under rule 62.1(a) and is based on an improper action or omission of a body other than the protest committee, a member of that body should not be a member of the protest committee.

## M3     THE HEARING

**M3.1**     Check the validity of the *protest* or request for redress.

- Are the contents adequate (rule 61.2 or 62)?

- Was it delivered in time? If not, is there good reason to extend the time limit (rule 61.3 or 62.2)?

- When required, was the protestor involved in or a witness to the incident (rule 60.1(a))?

- When necessary, was 'Protest' hailed and, if required, a red flag displayed correctly (rule 61.1(a))?

- When the flag or hail was not necessary, was the protestee informed?

- Decide whether the *protest* or request for redress is valid (rule 63.5).

- Once the validity of the *protest* or request has been determined, do not let the subject be introduced again unless truly new evidence is available.

**M3.2**     Take the evidence (rule 63.6).

- Ask the protestor and then the protestee to tell their stories. Then allow them to question one another. In a redress matter, ask the *party* to state the request.

- Invite questions from protest committee members.

- Make sure you know what facts each *party* is alleging before calling any witnesses. Their stories may be different.

- Allow anyone, including a boat's crew, to give evidence. It is the *party* who normally decides which witnesses to call, although the protest committee may also call witnesses (rule 63.6). The question asked by a *party* 'Would you like to hear N?' is best answered by 'It is your choice.'

- Call each *party's* witnesses (and the protest committee's if any) one by one. Limit *parties* to questioning the witness(es) (they may wander into general statements).

- Invite the protestee to question the protestor's witness first (and vice versa). This prevents the protestor from leading his witness from the beginning.

- Allow members of the protest committee who saw the incident to give evidence (rule 63.6), but only while the *parties* are present. Members who give evidence may be questioned, should take care to relate all they know about the incident that could affect the decision, and may remain on the protest committee (rule 63.3(a)).

- Try to prevent leading questions or hearsay evidence, but if that is impossible discount the evidence so obtained.

- Accept written evidence from a witness who is not available to be questioned only if all *parties* agree. In doing so they forego their rights to question that witness (rule 63.6).

- Ask one member of the committee to note down evidence, particularly times, distances, speeds, etc.

- Invite first the protestor and then the protestee to make a final statement of her case, particularly on any application or interpretation of the *rules*.

**M3.3**    Find the facts (rule 63.6).

- Write down the facts; resolve doubts one way or the other.

- Call back *parties* for more questions if necessary.

- When appropriate, draw a diagram of the incident using the facts you have found.

**M3.4**    Decide the *protest* or request for redress (rule 64).

- Base the decision on the facts found (if you cannot, find some more facts).

- In redress cases, make sure that no further evidence is needed from boats that will be affected by the decision.

**M3.5**    Inform the *parties* (rule 65).

- Recall the *parties* and read them the facts found, conclusions and *rules* that apply, and the decision. When time presses it is permissible to read the decision and give the details later.

- Give any *party* a copy of the decision on request. File the *protest* or request for redress with the committee records.

## M4     REOPENING A HEARING (rule 66)

**M4.1**   When a *party*, within the time limit, has asked for a hearing to be reopened, hear the *party* making the request, look at any video, etc., and decide whether there is any significant new evidence that might lead you to change your decision. Decide whether your interpretation of the *rules* may have been wrong; be open-minded as to whether you have made a mistake. If none of these applies refuse to reopen; otherwise schedule a hearing.

**M4.2**   Evidence is 'new';

- if it was not reasonably possible for the *party* asking for the reopening to have discovered the evidence before the original hearing,

- if the protest committee is satisfied that before the original hearing the evidence was diligently but unsuccessfully sought by the *party* asking for the reopening, or

- if the protest committee learns from any source that the evidence was not available to the *parties* at the time of the original hearing.

## M5     MISCONDUCT (rule 69)

**M5.1**   An action under this rule is not a *protest*, but the protest committee gives its allegations in writing to the competitor before the hearing. The hearing is conducted under rules similar to those governing a protest hearing but the protest committee must have at least three members (rule 69.2(a)). Use the greatest care to protect the competitor's rights.

**M5.2**   A competitor or a boat cannot protest under rule 69, but the protest form of a competitor who tries to do so may be accepted as a report to the protest committee, which can then decide whether or not to call a hearing.

**M5.3**   Unless World Sailing has appointed a person for the role, the protest committee may appoint a person to present the allegation. This person might be a race official, the person making the allegation or other appropriate person. When no reasonable alternative person is available, a person who was appointed as a member of the protest committee may present the allegation.

**M5.4**    When it is desirable to call a hearing under rule 69 as a result of a Part 2 incident, it is important to hear any boat-vs.-boat *protest* in the normal way, deciding which boat, if any, broke which *rule*, before proceeding against the competitor under rule 69.

**M5.5**    Although action under rule 69 is taken against a competitor, boat owner or *support person*, and not a boat, a boat may also be penalized (rules 69.2(h)(2) and 64.4).

**M5.6**    When a protest committee upholds a rule 69 allegation it will need to consider if it is appropriate to report to either a national authority or World Sailing. Guidance on when to report may be found in the World Sailing Case Book. When the protest committee does make a report it may recommend whether or not further action should be taken.

**M5.7**    Unless the right of appeal is denied in accordance with rule 70.5, a *party* to a rule 69 hearing may appeal the decision of the protest committee.

**M5.8**    Further guidance for protest committees about misconduct may be found on the World Sailing website.

**M6**    **APPEALS (rule 70 and Appendix R)**

When decisions can be appealed;

- retain the papers relevant to the hearing so that the information can easily be used for an appeal. Is there a diagram endorsed or prepared by the protest committee? Are the facts found sufficient? (Example: Was there an *overlap*? Yes or No. 'Perhaps' is not a fact found.) Are the names of the protest committee members and other important information on the form?

- comments by the protest committee on any appeal should enable the appeals committee to picture the whole incident clearly; the appeals committee knows nothing about the situation.

## M7    PHOTOGRAPHIC EVIDENCE

Photographs and videos can sometimes provide useful evidence but protest committees should recognize their limitations and note the following points:

- The *party* producing the photographic evidence is responsible for arranging the viewing.

- View the video several times to extract all the information from it.

- The depth perception of any single-lens camera is very poor; with a telephoto lens it is non-existent. When the camera views two *overlapped* boats at right angles to their course, it is impossible to assess the distance between them. When the camera views them head on, it is impossible to see whether an *overlap* exists unless it is substantial.

- Ask the following questions:

  - Where was the camera in relation to the boats?

  - Was the camera's platform moving? If so in what direction and how fast?

  - Is the angle changing as the boats approach the critical point? Fast panning causes radical change.

  - Did the camera have an unrestricted view throughout?

# APPENDIX N
## INTERNATIONAL JURIES

*See rules 70.5 and 91(b). This appendix shall not be changed by the notice of race, sailing instructions or national prescriptions.*

**N1 COMPOSITION, APPOINTMENT AND ORGANIZATION**

**N1.1** An international jury shall be composed of experienced sailors with excellent knowledge of the racing rules and extensive protest committee experience. It shall be independent of and have no members from the race committee, and be appointed by the organizing authority, subject to approval by the national authority if required (see rule 91(b)), or by World Sailing under rule 89.2(c).

**N1.2** The jury shall consist of a chairman, a vice chairman if desired, and other members for a total of at least five. A majority shall be International Judges.

**N1.3** No more than two members (three, in Groups M, N and Q) shall be from the same national authority.

**N1.4** (a) The chairman of a jury may appoint one or more panels composed in compliance with rules N1.1, N1.2 and N1.3. This can be done even if the full jury is not composed in compliance with these rules.

(b) The chairman of a jury may appoint panels of at least three members each, of which the majority shall be International Judges. Members of each panel shall be from at least three different national authorities except in Groups M, N and Q, where they shall be from at least two different national authorities. If dissatisfied with a panel's decision, a *party* is entitled to a hearing by a panel composed in compliance with rules N1.1, N1.2 and N1.3, except concerning the facts found, if requested within the time limit specified in the sailing instructions.

**N1.5** When a full jury, or a panel, has fewer than five members, because of illness or emergency, and no qualified replacements are available, it remains properly constituted if it consists of at least three members and if at least two of them are International Judges. When there are three or four members they shall be from at least three different national authorities except in Groups M, N and Q, where they shall be from at least two different national authorities.

**N1.6** When it is considered desirable that some members not participate in discussing and deciding a *protest* or request for redress, and no qualified replacements are available, the jury or panel remains properly constituted if at least three members remain and at least two of them are International Judges.

**N1.7** In exception to rules N1.1 and N1.2, World Sailing may in limited circumstances (see World Sailing Regulation 25.8.13) authorize an international jury consisting of a total of only three members. All members shall be International Judges. The members shall be from three different national authorities (two, in Groups M, N and Q). The authorization shall be stated in a letter of approval to the organizing authority and in the notice of race and sailing instructions, and the letter shall be posted on the event's official notice board.

**N1.8** When the national authority's approval is required for the appointment of an international jury (see rule 91(b)), notice of its approval shall be included in the sailing instructions or be posted on the official notice board.

**N1.9** If the jury or a panel acts while not properly constituted, its decisions may be appealed.

## N2    RESPONSIBILITIES

**N2.1** An international jury is responsible for hearing and deciding all *protests*, requests for redress and other matters arising under the rules of Part 5. When asked by the organizing authority or the race committee, it shall advise and assist them on any matter directly affecting the fairness of the competition.

**N2.2** Unless the organizing authority directs otherwise, the jury shall decide:

(a)  questions of eligibility, measurement or rating certificates; and
(b)  whether to authorize the substitution of competitors, boats or equipment when a *rule* requires such a decision.

**N2.3** The jury shall also decide matters referred to it by the organizing authority or the race committee.

**N3**    **PROCEDURES**

**N3.1**    Decisions of the jury, or of a panel, shall be made by a simple majority vote of all members. When there is an equal division of votes cast, the chairman of the meeting may cast an additional vote.

**N3.2**    Members shall not be regarded as having a significant *conflict of interest* (see rule 63.4) by reason of their nationality, club membership or similar. When otherwise considering a significant *conflict of interest* as required by rule 63.4, considerable weight must be given to the fact that decisions of an international jury cannot be appealed and this may affect the perception of fairness and lower the level of conflict that is significant. In case of doubt, the hearing should proceed as permitted by rule N1.6.

**N3.3**    If a panel fails to agree on a decision it may adjourn, in which case the chairman shall refer the matter to a properly constituted panel with as many members as possible, which may be the full jury.

**N4**    **MISCONDUCT (Rule 69)**

**N4.1**    World Sailing Regulation 35, Disciplinary Code, contains procedures that apply to specific international events with regard to the appointment of a person to conduct any investigation. These procedures override any conflicting provision of this appendix.

**N4.2**    A person shall be responsible for presenting to the hearing panel any allegations of misconduct under rule 69. This person shall not be a member of the hearing panel but may be a member of the jury. Such a person shall be required to make full disclosure of all material that may come into his possession in the course of his investigation to the person subject to allegations of a breach of rule 69.

**N4.3**    Prior to a hearing, the hearing panel, to the extent practically possible, shall not act as an investigator of any allegations made under rule 69. However, during the hearing the panel shall be entitled to ask any investigative questions it may see fit.

**N4.4**    If the panel decides to call a hearing, all material disclosed to the panel in order for them to make that decision must be disclosed to the person subject to the allegations before the hearing begins.

# APPENDIX P
# SPECIAL PROCEDURES
# FOR RULE 42

*All or part of this appendix applies only if the notice of race or sailing instructions so state.*

**P1**      **OBSERVERS AND PROCEDURE**

**P1.1**      The protest committee may appoint observers, including protest committee members, to act in accordance with rule P1.2. A person with a significant *conflict of interest* shall not be appointed as an observer.

**P1.2**      An observer appointed under rule P1.1 who sees a boat breaking rule 42 may penalize her by, as soon as reasonably possible, making a sound signal, pointing a yellow flag at her and hailing her sail number, even if she is no longer *racing*. A boat so penalized shall not be penalized a second time under rule 42 for the same incident.

**P2**      **PENALTIES**

**P2.1**      **First Penalty**

When a boat is first penalized under rule P1.2 her penalty shall be a Two-Turns Penalty under rule 44.2. If she fails to take it she shall be disqualified without a hearing.

**P2.2**      **Second Penalty**

When a boat is penalized a second time during the regatta, she shall promptly retire. If she fails to do so she shall be disqualified without a hearing and her score shall not be excluded.

**P2.3**      **Third and Subsequent Penalties**

When a boat is penalized a third or subsequent time during the regatta, she shall promptly retire. If she does so her penalty shall be disqualification without a hearing and her score shall not be excluded. If she fails to do so her penalty shall be disqualification without a hearing from all races in the regatta, with no score excluded, and the protest committee shall consider calling a hearing under rule 69.2.

**P2.4    Penalties Near the Finishing Line**

If a boat is penalized under rule P2.2 or P2.3 and it was not reasonably possible for her to retire before *finishing*, she shall be scored as if she had retired promptly.

**P3    POSTPONEMENT, GENERAL RECALL OR ABANDONMENT**

If a boat has been penalized under rule P1.2 and the race committee signals a *postponement*, general recall or *abandonment*, the penalty is cancelled, but it is still counted to determine the number of times she has been penalized during the regatta.

**P4    REDRESS LIMITATION**

A boat shall not be given redress for an action by a member of the protest committee or its designated observer under rule P1.2 unless the action was improper due to a failure to take into account a race committee signal or a class rule.

**P5    FLAGS O AND R**

**P5.1    When Rule P5 Applies**

Rule P5 applies if the class rules permit pumping, rocking and ooching when the wind speed exceeds a specified limit.

**P5.2    Before the Starting Signal**

(a)   The race committee may signal that pumping, rocking and ooching are permitted, as specified in the class rules, by displaying flag O before or with the warning signal.

(b)   If the wind speed becomes less than the specified limit after flag O has been displayed, the race committee may *postpone* the race. Then, before or with a new warning signal, the committee shall display either flag R, to signal that rule 42 as changed by the class rules applies, or flag O, as provided in rule P5.2(a).

(c)   If flag O or flag R is displayed before or with the warning signal, it shall be displayed until the starting signal.

177

**P5.3**    **After the Starting Signal**

After the starting signal,

(a)    if the wind speed exceeds the specified limit, the race committee may display flag O with repetitive sounds at a *mark* to signal that pumping, rocking and ooching are permitted, as specified in the class rules, after passing the *mark*;

(b)    if flag O has been displayed and the wind speed becomes less than the specified limit, the race committee may display flag R with repetitive sounds at a *mark* to signal that rule 42, as changed by the class rules, applies after passing the *mark*.

# APPENDIX R
## PROCEDURES FOR APPEALS AND REQUESTS

*See rule 70. A national authority may change this appendix by prescription but it shall not be changed by sailing instructions.*

**R1**    **APPEALS AND REQUESTS**

Appeals, requests by protest committees for confirmation or correction of their decisions, and requests for interpretations of the *rules* shall be made in compliance with this appendix.

**R2**    **SUBMISSION OF DOCUMENTS**

**R2.1**    To make an appeal,

(a)    no later than 15 days after receiving the protest committee's written decision or its decision not to reopen a hearing, the appellant shall send an appeal and a copy of the protest committee's decision to the national authority. The appeal shall state why the appellant believes the protest committee's decision or its procedures were incorrect;

(b)    when the hearing required by rule 63.1 has not been held within 30 days after a *protest* or request for redress was delivered, the appellant shall, within a further 15 days, send an appeal with a copy of the *protest* or request and any relevant correspondence. The national authority shall extend the time if there is good reason to do so;

(c)    when the protest committee fails to comply with rule 65, the appellant shall, within a reasonable time after the hearing, send an appeal with a copy of the *protest* or request and any relevant correspondence.

If a copy of the *protest* or request is not available, the appellant shall instead send a statement of its substance.

**R2.2**    The appellant shall also send, with the appeal or as soon as possible thereafter, all of the following documents that are available to her:

(a)    the written *protest(s)* or request(s) for redress;

(b)  a diagram, prepared or endorsed by the protest committee, showing the positions and tracks of all boats involved, the course to the next *mark* and the required side, the force and direction of the wind, and, if relevant, the depth of water and direction and speed of any current;

(c)  the notice of race, the sailing instructions, any other conditions governing the event, and any changes to them;

(d)  any additional relevant documents; and

(e)  the names, postal and email addresses, and telephone numbers of all *parties* to the hearing and the protest committee chairman.

**R2.3**   A request from a protest committee for confirmation or correction of its decision shall be sent no later than 15 days after the decision and shall include the decision and the documents listed in rule R2.2. A request for an interpretation of the *rules* shall include assumed facts.

**RYA**    *Note: An RYA Prescription (page 193) adds rule R2.4.*

**R3**     **RESPONSIBILITIES OF NATIONAL AUTHORITY AND PROTEST COMMITTEE**

Upon receipt of an appeal or a request for confirmation or correction, the national authority shall send to the *parties* and protest committee copies of the appeal or request and the protest committee's decision. It shall ask the protest committee for any relevant documents listed in rule R2.2 not sent by the appellant or the protest committee, and the protest committee shall promptly send them to the national authority. When the national authority has received them it shall send copies to the *parties*.

**R4**     **COMMENTS AND CLARIFICATIONS**

**R4.1**   The *parties* and protest committee may make comments on the appeal or request or on any of the documents listed in rule R2.2 by sending them in writing to the national authority.

**R4.2**   The national authority may seek clarifications of *rules* governing the event from organizations that are not *parties* to the hearing.

**R4.3**   The national authority shall send copies of comments and clarifications received to the *parties* and protest committee as appropriate.

**R4.4**     Comments on any document shall be made no later than 15 days after receiving it from the national authority.

**R5     INADEQUATE FACTS; REOPENING**

The national authority shall accept the protest committee's finding of facts except when it decides they are inadequate. In that case it shall require the committee to provide additional facts or other information, or to reopen the hearing and report any new finding of facts, and the committee shall promptly do so.

**R6     WITHDRAWING AN APPEAL**

An appellant may withdraw an appeal before it is decided by accepting the protest committee's decision.

# APPENDIX S
## STANDARD SAILING INSTRUCTIONS

*This appendix applies only if the notice of race so states.*

*These Standard Sailing Instructions may be used at an event in place of printed sailing instructions made available to each boat. To use them, state in the notice of race that 'The sailing instructions will consist of the instructions in RRS Appendix S, Standard Sailing Instructions, and supplementary sailing instructions that will be on the official notice board located at _____.'*

*The supplementary sailing instructions will include:*

1. *A table showing the schedule of races, including the day and date of each scheduled day of racing, the number of races scheduled each day, the scheduled time of the first warning signal each day, and the latest time for a warning signal on the last scheduled day of racing (see SI 5 below).*

2. *The location of the race office and of the flag pole on which signals made ashore will be displayed (SI 4.1).*

3. *A list of the marks that will be used and a description of each one (SI 8). How new marks will differ from original marks (SI 10).*

4. *The time limits, if any, that are listed in SI 12.*

5. *Any changes or additions to the instructions in this appendix.*

*A copy of the supplementary sailing instructions will be available to competitors on request.*

## SAILING INSTRUCTIONS

### 1     RULES

**1.1**     The regatta will be governed by the rules as defined in *The Racing Rules of Sailing*.

### 2     NOTICES TO COMPETITORS

**2.1**     Notices to competitors will be posted on the official notice board.

**2.2**     Supplementary sailing instructions (called 'the supplement' below) will be posted on the official notice board.

### 3     CHANGES TO SAILING INSTRUCTIONS

**3.1**     Any change to the sailing instructions will be posted before 0800 on the day it will take effect, except that any change to the schedule of races will be posted by 2000 on the day before it will take effect.

### 4     SIGNALS MADE ASHORE

**4.1**     Signals made ashore will be displayed from the flag pole. The supplement will state its location.

**4.2**     When flag AP is displayed ashore, '1 minute' is replaced with 'not less than 60 minutes' in the race signal AP.

### 5     SCHEDULE OF RACES

**5.1**     The supplement will include a table showing the days, dates, number of races scheduled, the scheduled times of the first warning signal each day, and the latest time for a warning signal on the last scheduled day of racing.

### 6     CLASS FLAGS

**6.1**     Each class flag will be the class insignia on a white background or as stated in the supplement.

### 7     THE COURSES

**7.1**     No later than the warning signal, the race committee will designate the course by displaying one or two letters followed by a number, and it may also display the approximate compass bearing of the first leg.

**7.2** The course diagrams are on the pages following SI 13. They show the courses, the order in which marks are to be passed, and the side on which each mark is to be left. The supplement may include additional courses.

## 8 MARKS

**8.1** A list of the marks that will be used, including a description of each one, will be included in the supplement.

## 9 THE START

**9.1** Races will be started by using RRS 26.

**9.2** The starting line will be between a staff displaying an orange flag on the race committee vessel and the course side of the starting mark.

## 10 CHANGE OF THE NEXT LEG OF THE COURSE

**10.1** To change the next leg of the course, the race committee will lay a new mark (or move the finishing line) and remove the original mark as soon as practicable. When in a subsequent change a new mark is replaced, it will be replaced by an original mark.

## 11 THE FINISH

**11.1** The finishing line will be between a staff displaying an orange flag on the race committee vessel and the course side of the finishing mark.

## 12 TIME LIMITS

**12.1** The supplement will state which of the following time limits, if any, will apply and, for each, the time limit.

- Mark 1 Time Limit    Time limit for the first boat to pass Mark 1.

- RaceTime Limit    Time limit for the first boat to sail the course and finish.

- Finishing Window    Time limit for boats to finish after the first boat sails the course and finishes.

**12.2** If no boat has passed Mark 1 within the Mark 1 Time Limit, the race shall be abandoned.

**12.3** Boats failing to finish within the Finishing Window shall be scored Did Not Finish without a hearing. This changes RRS 35, A4 and A5.

## 13    PROTESTS AND REQUESTS FOR REDRESS

**13.1**    Protest forms are available at the race office. Protests and requests for redress or reopening shall be delivered there within the appropriate time limit.

**13.2**    For each class, the protest time limit is 60 minutes after the last boat has finished the last race of the day or the race committee signals no more racing today, which ever is later.

**13.3**    Notices will be posted no later than 30 minutes after the protest time limit to inform competitors of hearings in which they are parties or named as witnesses and where the hearings will be held.

**13.4**    Notices of protests by the race committee, technical committee or protest committee will be posted to inform boats under RRS 61.1(b).

**13.5**    On the last scheduled day of racing a request for redress based on a protest committee decision shall be delivered no later than 30 minutes after the decision was posted. This changes RRS 62.2.

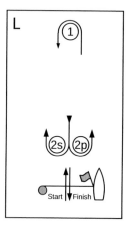

| Course L – Windward/Leeward, Leeward Finish | |
| --- | --- |
| *Signal* | *Mark Rounding Order* |
| L2 | Start – 1 – 2s/2p – 1 – Finish |
| L3 | Start – 1 – 2s/2p – 1 – 2s/2p – 1 – Finish |
| L4 | Start – 1 – 2s/2p – 1 – 2s/2p – 1 – 2s/2p – 1 – Finish |

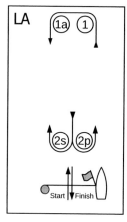

| Course LA – Windward/Leeward with Offset Mark, Leeward Finish | |
| --- | --- |
| *Signal* | *Mark Rounding Order* |
| LA2 | Start – 1 – 1a – 2s/2p – 1 – 1a – Finish |
| LA3 | Start – 1 – 1a – 2s/2p – 1 – 1a – 2s/2p – 1 – 1a – Finish |
| LA4 | Start – 1 – 1a – 2s/2p – 1 – 1a – 2s/2p – 1 – 1a – 2s/2p – 1 – 1a – Finish |

| Course W – Windward/Leeward, Windward Finish ||
| Signal | Mark Rounding Order |
| --- | --- |
| W2 | Start – 1 – 2s/2p – Finish |
| W3 | Start – 1 – 2s/2p – 1 – 2s/2p – Finish |
| W4 | Start – 1 – 2s/2p – 1 – 2s/2p – 1 – 2s/2p – Finish |

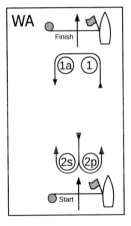

| Course WA – Windward/Leeward with Offset Mark, Windward Finish ||
| Signal | Mark Rounding Order |
| --- | --- |
| WA2 | Start – 1 – 1a - 2s/2p – Finish |
| WA3 | Start – 1 – 1a – 2s/2p – 1 – 1a - 2s/2p – Finish |
| WA4 | Start – 1 – 1a – 2s/2p – 1 – 1a – 2s/2p – 1 – 1a – 2s/2p – Finish |

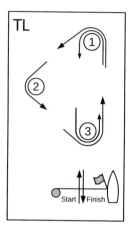

| Course TL – Triangle, Leeward Finish | |
| --- | --- |
| *Signal* | *Mark Rounding Order* |
| TL2 | Start – 1 – 2 – 3 – 1 – Finish |
| TL3 | Start – 1 – 2 – 3 – 1 – 3 – 1 – Finish |
| TL4 | Start – 1 – 2 – 3 – 1 – 3 – 1 – 3 – 1 – Finish |

| Course TW – Triangle, Windward Finish | |
| --- | --- |
| *Signal* | *Mark Rounding Order* |
| TW2 | Start – 1 – 2 – 3 – Finish |
| TW3 | Start – 1 – 2 – 3 – 1 – 3 – Finish |
| TW4 | Start – 1 – 2 – 3 – 1 – 3 – 1 – 3 – Finish |

# APPENDIX T
## ARBITRATION

*Appendix T can be found in the World Sailing Racing Rules of Sailing which can be downloaded from **sailing.org/racingrules/ documents***

*The appendix applies only if the notice of race or sailing instructions so state.*

*The appendix should be used in accordance with the guidance on arbitration that can be found in the World Sailing International Judges Manual, which can be downloaded from the World Sailing website.*

---

*An alternative is the RYA Rules Disputes Procedures which have been used throughout the UK for over a decade and may be more useful at events at or below National Championship level. The procedures can be found at **rya.org.uk/racingrules** or at **rya.org.uk/go/rulesdisputes**. The procedures include the simple notice of race sentence which is necessary to implement RYA Arbitration.*

# PRESCRIPTIONS

*With effect from 1 January 2017, the RYA prescribes*

**Rule**

### 3 Acceptance of the Rules

Add new rule 3.6: 'Each competitor and boat owner shall ensure that their *support persons* comply with the *rules*.'

### 5 Anti-Doping

The national authority procedural rules required by World Sailing regulation 21.16 to implement the World Anti-Doping Code through World Sailing Regulation 21 are the **RYA Anti-Doping Rules**, as published on the RYA website.

### 40 Personal Flotation Devices

When a *rule* requires a personal flotation device to be worn, the device shall comply with the specifications for the personal flotation devices that the boat is required to carry. If more than one specification applies, the personal flotation device worn shall comply with the highest of them.

### 50.4 Headsails

For the purposes of rules 50 and 54 and Appendix G, the difference between a headsail and a spinnaker is that, for a headsail, the distance measured between its **half leech point** and its **half luff point**, is less than 75% of its **foot length**. A sail tacked down behind the **foremost mast** is not a headsail.

Terms in **bold** are as defined in the Equipment Rules of Sailing.

### 67 Damages

1. Any issue of liability or claim for damages arising from an incident while a boat is bound by *The Racing Rules of Sailing* shall be subject to the jurisdiction of the courts and not considered by a protest committee.

2. A boat that takes a penalty or retires does not thereby admit liability for damages or that she has broken a *rule*.

**70.5** **Right of Appeal**

1. RYA approval is not required to deny the right of appeal under rule 70.5(a).

2. The RYA will not consider approving the denial of the right of appeal under rule 70.5(b) unless

   (a) the event is open only to boats entered by an organization affiliated to the RYA, a member of such an organization or a personal member of the RYA;

   (b) the RYA decides there is good reason to approve; the cost of an international jury which would otherwise be appropriate for the event is not a good reason;

   (c) the protest committee is approved by the RYA; and

   (d) application to the RYA is made no later than one month before the notice of race is to be issued. In exceptional circumstances, the RYA may consider a later application.

   A copy of the RYA letter of approval shall be displayed on the official notice board.

   However, the denial of appeal shall not apply to a party to a hearing under rule 69.2, Misconduct, but the decision of the protest committee shall determine the results of the event.

**78** **Compliance with Class Rules; Certificates**
A race committee or technical committee may inspect or measure any **boat** or **personal equipment**, at any time.

Terms in **bold** are as defined in the Equipment Rules of Sailing.

**86.3** **Rule Changes**
An organizing authority wishing to develop or test alternative racing rules shall obtain prior approval from the RYA. An application form is available from the RYA. The notice of race shall include the approved alternative rules. The organizing authority shall promptly report the results of the development or test to the RYA.

**88.2** **Changes to National Authority Prescriptions**
Notices of race and sailing instructions shall not change a prescription of the RYA. However, when an international jury has been appointed for an event, only the prescriptions to rules 3, 5, 67, 86.3 and 88.2 shall apply.

## APPENDIX G   IDENTIFICATION ON SAILS

### G1   Identification, Specifications, Positioning

The requirements of rules G1.1, G1.2 and G1.3 apply to all British owned boats except that:

1. under rule G1.1(a), class insignia need not be carried when the boat carries a sail number from one of the series specified in prescription G2-1, G2-2, G2-3 or G2-4 below;

2. under rule G1.1(c), a sail number of more than four digits may be carried;

3. under rule G1.1(c), for boats other than World Sailing classes, one of the authorities specified in G2 below shall allot an appropriate sail number;

4. under rule G1.2(b), the height of a letter included as part of a sail number shall be the same as any numerals included in the sail number;

5. under rule G1.3(c), the national letters may be placed in front of or above the sail numbers.

### G2   Series of Sail Numbers and Issuing Authorities Approved by the RYA:

1. Y, M, N, T, A, L and X series issued by the RYA.

2. R series issued by the Royal Ocean Racing Club.

3. C series issued by the Clyde Yacht Clubs Association.

4. National class series issued by the RYA.

5. Series issued by RYA affiliated class associations and approved by the RYA.

6. Series issued by a builder of a new class and approved by the RYA.

## APPENDIX R   PROCEDURES FOR APPEALS AND REQUESTS

### R2.1   Submission of Appeal

Rule R2.1 shall apply except as changed by the following:

1. The appellant shall notify RYA Racing stating an intention to appeal within the relevant time limit in rule R2.1. No details are needed at this stage.

2. Within 15 days thereafter, the appellant shall send to the RYA a completed appeal form with a copy of the protest committee's decision and other documents listed in rule R2.2, all as far as reasonably possible.

3. Unless the appellant is a personal member of the RYA, an appeal fee, stated on the appeal form, is payable to the RYA and shall be sent with the appeal form.

The appeal form is available from www.rya.org.uk/racingrules or by request to RYA Racing.

## R2.4 Failure to Comply with Procedures for Appeal or Request

Add new rule R2.4:

If the appellant does not comply with rule R2.1 as prescribed or the protest committee does not comply with rule R2.3, the RYA will refuse to hear the appeal unless there are exceptional circumstances. If other parties to the protest or the protest committee do not meet the requirements of the procedure, the RYA may decide the appeal as it thinks fit.

## WORLD SAILING REGULATION 20 ADVERTISING CODE

### 20.2.3 Right to Display Advertising on a Boat

When the right to display advertising on a boat is subject to prior authorisation by the national authority in accordance with regulation 20.2.3.3, the approval of the RYA is automatically granted provided that such advertising is permitted by the relevant rules of the class, rating system or handicapping system.

### 20.8.2 Fees

When the person in charge of a boat chooses to display advertising, the RYA will not impose a fee as permitted by regulation 20.8.2.

*NOTE*

*The RYA prescription to rule 88.2 was approved by World Sailing on 26 July 2016.*

# RACING RULES GUIDANCE

Under the umbrella of its Racing Charter, the RYA provides guidance on the Racing Rules of Sailing. The guidance offered is the opinion of experts and is not a binding interpretation of the rules, nor will it be appropriate for all racing. Comments or questions are welcome and should be made by email to the RYA at racingrules@rya.org.uk.

1    GUIDANCE BOOKLETS

The RYA has produced two guidance books which are available free of charge on the World Sailing racing rules of sailing, a partnership between World Sailing and the RYA – see www.rya.org.uk/go/wsapp, the RYA website at www.rya.org.uk/racingrules, or by clicking at www.rya.org.uk/go/RRSguidance. The books are available as eBooks or as PDF files – eBooks are recommended as they provide automatic notification of updates.

RYA CASE BOOK

The RYA Case Book contains illustrative and persuasive, but not binding, interpretations and explanations of the rules.

RYA RACING RULES GUIDANCE

This book, which contains three categories of guidance:

- General Guidance
- RYA Rules Disputes Procedures
- Guidance Primarily for Race Officials

The books will be updated as required, but at least annually in December. Additions and changes between updates are published on the RYA's website.

2    ADVISORY SERVICES

The RYA also provides advisory services. The RYA Racing Rules Committee provides an advisory service to help individuals, protest committees, clubs, classes and other organisations with their interpretation of the racing rules. This is intended to offer prompt informal advice without the delays inherent in a formal appeal. The RYA Race Management Committee provides advice on race management issues, including the writing of notices of race and sailing instructions.

3    RYA RACING RULES GUIDANCE BOOKLET

At end 2017 the RYA Racing Rules Guidance book contained the following guidance:

## GENERAL GUIDANCE

### Advertising

An explanation of who may choose advertising for a boat, sailboard or clothing at an event; how class rules, rating systems and handicapping systems may vary advertising rules, and the reservations for advertising by event sponsors.

### Appeals and Requests for Confirmation or Correction

Questions and answers about the appeals and requests processes; includes the RYA Appeal Form.

### Boats with Limited Visibility

Addressed primarily to boats with asymmetric spinnakers, the paper explains the obligations of such boats and of other boats sailing in the vicinity.

### Changes to the Racing Rules from January 2017

The main changes to the Racing Rules of Sailing effective from January 2017.

### Outside Help

Emphasises that everyone is required to give help to any person or boat that may be in danger, and that the recipient of such help does not necessarily break racing rule 41 which limits the help a boat may receive.

### Racing Under the IRPCAS
Guidance about racing under the International Regulations for Preventing Collisions at Sea (IRPCAS), the effect of Traffic Separation Schemes on race management and competitors, and the differences between the racing rules and the IRPCAS.

### Redress
Guidance about what and when redress can and cannot be given.

### Small Boat Safety Regulations
Recommended safety regulations for inshore racing for dinghies and small keelboats.

### Information for Support Persons
Guidance (on one page, to facilitate handing it out) for people who may be classified as a '*Support Person*' as defined in the RRS 2017-2020. This definition includes a parent or guardian, a coach, a medical or paramedical practitioner, a boat maintainer, a personal assistant to a disabled competitor or any other person working with or assisting a sailor prepare for or compete in a race.

## RYA RULES DISPUTES PROCEDURES

### Protest Form
For protests and requests for redress, including arbitration under the RYA Rules Disputes procedures.

### Hearing Decision Form
An electronic form for protest committees, and arbitrators under the RYA Rules Disputes procedures, to record the proceedings and decisions of a hearing (replaces page 2 of the RYA Protest Form).

### Rules Disputes
About the use of the exoneration penalty, advisory hearings and RYA arbitration.

### Rules Disputes Questions and Answers
Frequently asked questions that arise when advisory hearings or arbitration are adopted.

### Rules Disputes Poster
A diagrammatic guide to the RYA Rules Disputes process.

## GUIDANCE PRIMARILY FOR RACE OFFICIALS

### Competitors Retiring or Withdrawing a Retirement

Guidance for race committees on time limits for competitors retiring or withdrawing a retirement.

### Discretionary Penalties

Guidance on discretionary penalties which are becoming increasingly common for a breach of some rules.

### Environmental Responsibility and Trash Disposal

Guidance on the Basic Principle, Environmental Responsibility, and rule 55, Trash Disposal.

### GPS Evidence in Hearings

Guidance on a technical area that is becoming more common.

### IRC Rating Protests

Guidance on protests concerning alleged breaches of IRC measurement rules (should be read in conjunction with the RYA guidance on Measurement Protests below).

### Measurement Protests

Guidance on protests concerning alleged breaches of measurement rules. It does not directly address protests concerning other aspects of class rules, although some of the principles are applicable to such protests.

### Permitting Use of an Engine

Options for, and limits on, sailing instructions allowing the use of an engine for propulsion.

### Protecting Boats Before the Start

Methods and penalties to inhibit interference by boats that are not racing with boats that are in their starting sequence.

### Protecting Committee Boats

The paper explains the correct methods for race managers to protect their own and borrowed boats used as committee boats.

### Recommendations for Protest Committees
Extended guidance on Appendix M regarding protest committee procedure with examples of appropriate actions in described circumstances.

### Restricting Protests or Requests for Redress by Boats
Guidance on the limited number of circumstances where it is good practice to restrict protests by boats. Restriction of requests for redress by boats is not recommended.

### Risk Management
Guidance on a 'Risk Statement' recommended by the RYA to replace a 'Disclaimer of Liability' in Notices of Race and Sailing Instructions. The recommendation can be found in Appendix J, Addendum A (RYA), on page 137.

### Scoring
Guidance on the application and operation of RRS Appendix A, Scoring.

### Starting Penalties
Describes alternatives to returning to start correctly for boats that are over the starting line at the starting signal (OCS).

### Virtual Protest Committee Hearings
Guidance on protest and redress hearings held by email, teleconference or video (virtual hearings).

### 4  MISCONDUCT
Further to the above, outline guidance on the application of racing rules 2 and 69, together with possible actions, is on page 200.

In addition, World Sailing has produced a booklet, 'Misconduct Guidance', which is available at www.sailing.org/racingrules/documents.

### 5  OTHER RYA RACING RULES PUBLICATIONS
Other RYA racing rules publications and eBooks are available to purchase from the RYA shop at www.rya.org.uk/shop.

# MISCONDUCT

Rule 69 is used by the sport of sailboat racing to control and penalise unacceptable behaviour during an event. It covers both on and off-the-water behaviour. Action under rule 69 is entirely separate from any protest and from any penalty for any other rule that may have been broken.

The protest committee may receive reports from competitors, officials or spectators, or may initiate action of its own accord. It may decide merely to interview the competitor, or to act under rule 69.2. If proceeding with a rule 69.2 hearing, the protest committee must promptly inform the competitor in writing of the alleged misconduct.

Allegations have to be proven to the comfortable satisfaction of the protest committee, bearing in mind the seriousness of the allegations. Competitors subject to a rule 69 hearing are entitled to be accompanied by a friend, coach, parent or other advisor at the hearing.

If the protest committee decides that the competitor did commit the alleged misconduct, it may take a range of action as set out in rules 69.2(h). Rule 69.2 explains when a report should be made to the RYA which, when appropriate, may then impose further penalties beyond the jurisdiction of the protest committee.

The following levels of action are among those available to a protest committee after consideration of a rule 69 report. Level 1 to 5 actions are only possible after a hearing:

| Misconduct Level | Possible Action |
|---|---|
| 0 | Interview with competitor, but no hearing and so no penalty is possible |
| 1 | Warning, but no penalty |
| 2 | Increase the boat's score |
| | Exclude competitor and, when appropriate, disqualify the boat: |
| 3 | - from one or more races |
| 4 | - from the event |
| 5 | - from the event and recommend further action by the RYA |

In certain circumstances, competitors and their boats can be penalised for the misconduct of their support persons. The circumstances in which this can be done are set out in rule 69.2(i).

Protest committees are advised to review World Sailing's Misconduct Guidance, which contains further guidance on recommended penalties for misconduct.

In addition to rule 69, the protest committee may take other action within its jurisdiction. This may include hearing protests under rule 2 (Fair Sailing) which can be lodged by a boat, the race committee or the protest committee itself. The protest committee may also disqualify a boat under rule 2 during any other protest hearing if it is satisfied the boat has clearly violated the recognized principles of sportsmanship and fair play.

# TIME AND SPEED CHARTS

## Time in seconds to advance 1 length

| Boat Speed Knots | Length of Yacht in Metres | | | | | | |
|---|---|---|---|---|---|---|---|
| | 4 | 5 | 6 | 7 | 8 | 9 | 10 |
| 1 | 7.8 | 9.7 | 11.7 | 13.6 | 15.5 | 17.5 | 19.4 |
| 2 | 3.9 | 4.9 | 5.8 | 6.8 | 7.8 | 8.7 | 9.7 |
| 3 | 2.6 | 3.2 | 3.9 | 4.5 | 5.2 | 5.8 | 6.5 |
| 4 | 1.9 | 2.4 | 2.9 | 3.4 | 3.9 | 4.4 | 4.9 |
| 5 | 1.6 | 1.9 | 2.3 | 2.7 | 3.1 | 3.5 | 3.9 |
| 6 | 1.3 | 1.6 | 1.9 | 2.3 | 2.6 | 2.9 | 3.2 |
| 7 | 1.1 | 1.4 | 1.7 | 1.9 | 2.2 | 2.5 | 2.8 |
| 8 | 1.0 | 1.2 | 1.5 | 1.7 | 1.9 | 2.2 | 2.4 |
| 9 | 0.9 | 1.1 | 1.3 | 1.5 | 1.7 | 1.9 | 2.2 |
| 10 | 0.8 | 1.0 | 1.2 | 1.4 | 1.6 | 1.7 | 1.9 |

1 knot = 0.515 m/sec = 1.666ft/sec

## Boat velocities for given wind speeds

This table gives approximations only. Velocities are for non-planing boats that are reaching or running. For beating, velocities will be lower and multiplying by 0.8 will yield an approximate result.

| Wind | | Waterline length of boat in metres | | | | | | | | | | | | |
|---|---|---|---|---|---|---|---|---|---|---|---|---|---|---|
| | | 3 | | 4 | | 5 | | 6 | | 7 | | 8 | | 9 | |
| Kn | Bft | Kn | m/sec | Kn | m/sec | Kn | m/sec | Kn | m/sec | Kn | m/sec | Kn | m/sec | Kn | m/sec |
| 1 | 1 | 0.2 | 0.1 | 0.2 | 0.1 | 0.2 | 0.1 | 0.2 | 0.1 | 0.3 | 0.1 | 0.3 | 0.1 | 0.4 | 0.2 |
| 2 | | 0.4 | 0.2 | 0.5 | 0.2 | 0.4 | 0.2 | 0.4 | 0.2 | 0.5 | 0.3 | 0.7 | 0.3 | 0.8 | 0.4 |
| 3 | | 0.7 | 0.4 | 0.6 | 0.3 | 0.7 | 0.4 | 0.7 | 0.3 | 0.8 | 0.4 | 1.0 | 0.5 | 1.2 | 0.6 |
| 4 | 2 | 0.9 | 0.5 | 0.9 | 0.5 | 0.9 | 0.5 | 0.9 | 0.5 | 1.1 | 0.6 | 1.3 | 0.7 | 1.6 | 0.8 |
| 5 | | 1.1 | 0.6 | 1.1 | 0.6 | 1.1 | 0.6 | 1.1 | 0.6 | 1.4 | 0.7 | 1.7 | 0.9 | 2.0 | 1.0 |
| 6 | | 1.4 | 0.7 | 1.4 | 0.7 | 1.4 | 0.7 | 1.4 | 0.7 | 1.7 | 0.9 | 2.1 | 1.1 | 2.4 | 1.3 |
| 7 | 3 | 1.6 | 0.8 | 1.6 | 0.8 | 1.6 | 0.8 | 1.6 | 0.8 | 2.0 | 1.0 | 2.4 | 1.2 | 2.8 | 1.5 |
| 11 | 4 | 2.5 | 1.3 | 2.6 | 1.3 | 2.6 | 1.3 | 2.6 | 1.3 | 3.1 | 1.6 | 3.8 | 2.0 | 4.5 | 2.3 |
| 17 | 5 | 4.0 | 2.0 | 3.9 | 2.0 | 4.0 | 2.1 | 4.1 | 2.1 | 4.9 | 2.5 | 5.9 | 3.0 | 6.9 | 3.6 |
| 22 | 6 | 5.2 | 2.7 | 5.1 | 2.6 | 5.1 | 2.6 | 5.3 | 2.7 | 6.3 | 3.2 | 7.7 | 4.0 | 9.0 | 4.7 |

1 metre = 3.281 feet

# BEAUFORT SCALE

| Wind | | | | | |
|---|---|---|---|---|---|
| Bft | Kn | Km/hr | m/sec | ft/sec | |
| 1 | 1 | 1.85 | 0.51 | 1.69 | Light air, ripples |
| | 2 | 3.71 | 103 | 3.38 | |
| | 3 | 5.56 | 1.54 | 5.07 | |
| 2 | 4 | 7.41 | 2.06 | 6.76 | Light breeze, small wavelets |
| | 5 | 9.27 | 2.57 | 8.44 | |
| | 6 | 11.12 | 3.09 | 10.13 | |
| 3 | 7 | 12.97 | 3.60 | 11.82 | Gentle breeze, large wavelets |
| | 8 | 14.82 | 4.12 | 13.51 | |
| | 9 | 16.68 | 4.63 | 15.20 | |
| | 10 | 18.53 | 5.15 | 16.89 | |
| 4 | 11 | 20.38 | 5.66 | 18.58 | Moderate breeze, small waves, frequent white horses |
| | 12 | 22.24 | 6.18 | 20.27 | |
| | 13 | 24.09 | 6.69 | 21.96 | |
| | 14 | 25.94 | 7.21 | 23.64 | |
| | 15 | 27.80 | 7.72 | 25.33 | |
| | 16 | 29.65 | 8.24 | 27.02 | |
| 5 | 17 | 31.50 | 8.75 | 28.71 | Fresh breeze, moderate waves, white horses. |
| | 18 | 33.36 | 9.27 | 30.40 | |
| | 19 | 35.21 | 9.78 | 32.09 | |
| | 20 | 37.06 | 10.29 | 33.78 | |
| | 21 | 38.91 | 10.81 | 35.47 | |
| 6 | 22 | 40.77 | 11.32 | 37.16 | Strong breeze, foaming crests |
| | 23 | 42.62 | 11.84 | 38.84 | |
| | 24 | 44.47 | 12.35 | 40.53 | |
| | 25 | 46.33 | 12.87 | 42.22 | |

# RACE SIGNALS

The meanings of visual and sound signals are stated below. An arrow pointing up or down (↑ ↓) means that a visual signal is displayed or removed. A dot (●) means a sound; five short dashes ( ▬ ▬ ▬ ▬ ▬ ) mean repetitive sounds. A long dash (▬▬) means a long sound. When a visual signal is displayed over a class flag, the signal applies only to that class.

## Postponement Signals

↑ ●●    ↓ ●

### AP
Races not started are *postponed*. The warning signal will be made 1 minute after removal unless at that time the race is *postponed* again or *abandoned*.

↑ ●●

↑ ●●    ↓ ●

**AP over H**
Races not started are *postponed*. Further signals ashore.

**AP over A**
Races not started are *postponed*. No more racing today.

**AP over a numeral pennant**
Hours *postponement* from the scheduled starting time.

## Abandonment Signals

↑ ●●●    ↓ ●

### N
All races that have started are *abandoned*. Return to the starting area. The warning signal will be made 1 minute after removal unless at that time the race is *abandoned* again or *postponed*.

↑ ●●●

**N over H**
All races are *abandoned*. Further signals ashore.

↑ ●●●

**N over A**
All races are *abandoned*. No more racing today.